Endorsements

Gordon Anderson—President, North Central Bible College, Minneapolis, Minnesota

James Davis has distinguished himself through many years of field ministry as an evangelist and as the National Evangelists Representative for the Assemblies of God. In his role as National Evangelists Representative he has provided outstanding leadership for the evangelists and has brought together many different elements within the constituency to draw attention to evangelistic work. Now, as an author, he is making an enormous contribution to the understanding of the work and role of the evangelist. I appreciate James Davis and commend this work to anyone who is interested in learning more about the role of the evangelist and evangelism in the local church.

Ron Auch—Author, Evangelist, Racine, Wisconsin

I believe that *The Pastor's Best Friend: The New Testament Evangelist* is long overdue. When I think back to my Bible college experiences I realize that nothing was taught about the importance or role of an evangelist. A book like this one could easily become the evangelist's "bible."

Tommy Barnett—Pastor, First Assembly of God, Phoenix, Arizona

This book should be required reading. In a world full of distractions and diversions, this work focuses in on the very reasons anyone should go into ministry, that is, winning the lost, building local churches, equipping the saints, and exalting Jesus Christ. It is my hope that multitudes will be touched and inspired while being equipped to be great soul-winners for the glory of God. Thank God for a reemphasis on the vital role of New Testament evangelist.

M. Wayne Benson—Pastor, First Assembly of God, Grand Rapids, Michigan

The message of this book is a two-edged sword elevating the evangelist and evangelism to the place they both must have for the world to be reached for Christ. It is a message that every pastor and evangelist should have, and it comes from the heart of an anointed evangelist who understands both the evangelist—his calling, his ministry, and his message—and the true meaning of evangelism. James Davis reminds us that the evangelist is an ambassador, anointed to proclaim revival. More than being on the cutting-edge of personal soul-winning, the evangelist is multigifted, and his "work of service" or "ministry" is for "equipping for evangelism." He sets the standard in ethics, excellence, and effectiveness in evangelism as being the main function of the church. This book is a challenge to every pastor and evangelist for the river of revival to sweep America!

Warren Benson—Vice President of Professional Doctoral Programs, Professor of Christian Education, Trinity Evangelical Divinity School, Deerfield, Illinois

This book is biblically principled, hermeneutically credible, experientially realistic, and eminently tender toward the work of the Spirit in the evangelistic task. *The Pastor's Best Friend: The New Testament Evangelist* emerges out of the crucible of eighteen years of proven ministry. Read slowly and with an openness of heart, it could mark your ministry for decades.

Robert D. Crabtree—District Superintendent, Columbus, Ohio

Evangelist James Davis has produced this valuable book as a result of his own experiences as an evangelist, as well as the results of useful research and pertinent surveys. Pastors as well as evangelists should read this book! The book ties the biblical with the practical through clear-cut applications. It is very instructional, well-documented, and inspirational. This book is a must for you to read if you believe God has called you to be an evangelist.

Dennis A. Davis—President, Northwest College of the Assemblies of God, Kirkland, Washington

James Davis has captured in one volume the history of, the biblical base for, a description and calling of, and the work and life of the evangelist. This book will help anyone giving a careful look at the evangelist to solidify one's calling, to prepare for the task in every area, and to gain a clearer understanding of this vital ministry gift. This is must reading for every pastor and evangelist in their desire for effective evangelistic ministry in the local church.

Richard Dresselhaus—Pastor, First Assembly of God, San Diego, California

Here is a biblically sound, well-written, comprehensive book for all those who have a heart for evangelism. The uninitiated as well as the well-seasoned will find here the kind of material which will give understanding, focus, and motivation for this vital and essential ministry within the local church. The challenge of the twenty-first century makes this book of special relevance.

Sam Farina—Evangelist, Racine, Wisconsin

Recent revival and spiritual awakening have made this book incredibly timely. Reading this book refreshed my heart, renewed my love for souls, and brought me back to the one grand focus of ministry—*evangelism!*

Wayde I. Goodall—National Coordinator, Ministerial Enrichment for the Assemblies of God, Executive Editor, *Enrichment* Journal, Springfield, Missouri

I am thrilled with the outstanding work that James Davis has done in his book on evangelism—not only is a book on this topic a rarity for the Assemblies of God, but for the Pentecostal world as well. His work is thorough, to the point, full of solid theological truth, and will be a tremendous encouragement to any evangelist or minister. He has done his homework on this critical subject. This work has been needed for a long time, and I am sure it will prove to make a mark on one of the most powerful ministries in the Church today.

Delmar R. Guynes—President, Southwestern Assemblies of God University, Waxahachie, Texas

James Davis has done a great service to the Church's ministry of evangelism by his focus and diligent research efforts in the production of this book for evangelists. The greatest possible expression of the evangelistic gift is that which inspires and prepares the entire Church body for evangelistic ministry. James Davis has done this well in this book. It will prove to be a challenging study for ministers and laypersons alike, and I recommend it heartily.

James L. Hennesy—President, Southeastern College, Lakeland, Florida

As we move into the twenty-first century it is clearly evident that the office of the evangelist is being restored to the Church. A guide that is both practical and inspirational is necessary if the church is to reap the maximum benefits through evangelistic endeavors. The Lord of the Harvest has directed James Davis in providing the Church with such a book. Ministers in all offices of the church, including pastors and evangelists, will be richly rewarded by carefully digesting the truths found in this book.

Stephen Hill—Missionary Evangelist, Brownsville Assembly of God, Pensacola, Florida

James Davis is a man after God's own heart. His burning desire for the lost to be saved, along with his personal pursuit of holiness, has placed him in the forefront of worldwide evangelism. This valuable manuscript will be used of the Lord to ignite a fire in the hearts of God's soldiers. May it be an instrument in God's hands to raise up more holy evangelists, which will in turn result in the conversion of millions of souls, extending God's kingdom around the globe.

Stanley M. Horton—General Editor, Logion Textbooks, Springfield, Missouri

James Davis shows the centrality of Spirit-gifted, Christ-centered evangelism in the plan of God for the Church. Bible college students and young Pentecostal evangelists will find in the book the tools they need for successfully spreading the gospel in fulfillment of the Great Commission. Pastors will gain a better understanding of their relationship to the evangelist. Hopefully, many will read the book and the Holy Spirit will use it to help open their minds and hearts to the call of God to a difficult but most-needed ministry.

Daniel E. Johnson—Author, Evangelist, Tacoma, Washington

Despite a lifetime of ministry and study I was unaware of the extensive and detailed definition of the evangelist and description of his life and times. It's hard to believe that we have waited so long for such a book. It makes a compelling case for the role of the biblical evangelist. It ought to be required reading in every Bible college and seminary.

Sam Johnson—Missionary Evangelist, Charlotte, North Carolina

There is in every lifetime a moment of great opportunity. James Davis has seized that moment with his timely book, *The Pastor's Best Friend: The New Testament Evangelist.* As the revival fires flame across America and the world, the author tells us how to maximize the ministry of the evangelist, and for that, we are eternally grateful.

David L. Larsen—Author, Professor Emeritus of Preaching, Trinity Evangelical Divinity School, Deerfield, Illinois

The winds of the Spirit are blowing around the world and this means a renewal of interest in doing the "work of the evangelist" in the local church and in the ministry of evangelists in the entire Church. James Davis has given us a biblical, sound, and practical book for evangelists which should be studied by pastors and laypeople who are burdened for the lost. This fine work is a model for other denominational fellowships.

John Lindell—Pastor, James River Assembly of God, Springfield, Missouri

Few works exist on the role and the importance of the evangelist. In a concise, yet comprehensive manner, James Davis offers both biblical definition and practical application of what it means to be an evangelist. You can count on it—this volume will be a classic for decades to come on the ministry of the evangelist.

Lowell Lundstrom—Evangelist, Sisseton, South Dakota

James Davis's book is a must read for every person sincerely interested in evangelism. This book should be required reading for every Bible college that is serious about preparing evangelists for Kingdom service. This scholarly work is relevant, thorough, and practical. It is full of great quotes, tips, and helpful diagrams. James Davis includes nearly two hundred references from such greats as E. M. Bounds, Bill Bright, Robert Coleman, Charles Finney, Billy Graham, Howard Hendricks, Ron Hutchcraft, John MacArthur, John Maxwell, John R. W. Stott, George Sweeting, R. A. Torrey, Dennis Waitley, and Warren Wiersbe. Chapter 10, "The Practics of the Evangelist," is worth the whole book. As an evangelist of forty years, it took me a long time to realize I was a small business like this chapter describes. Read it and save yourself fifteen years of learning through experience.

Don Meyer—President, Valley Forge Christian College, Phoenix, Arizona

Anyone who cares about the ministry of the evangelist should read this work by veteran evangelist James Davis. He speaks out of the depths of his own life experiences and serious research.

Included here are insights on the theology, history, administration, homiletics, spirituality, and everyday life of the evangelist. Although this book has been written in the milieu of Assemblies of God evangelistic ministry, the principles are transdenominational. What a helpful resource this will be for all who are involved in the Kingdom—especially evangelists.

Stephen Olford—Author, Founder and Senior Lecturer of the Stephen Olford Center for Biblical Preaching in Memphis, Tennessee

As an evangelist, I heartily welcome and recommend James Davis's book on evangelism. While much has been written on this subject over the years, nothing has appeared recently to compare with this well-researched book. It is both comprehensive and concise, biblical and practical, spiritual and personal. It is written by an evangelist for evangelists and for pastors who wish to do the "work of the evangelist."

John Palmer—Pastor, First Assembly of God, Des Moines, Iowa

This book is awesome! Using three beautiful threads—the thread of Scriptural truth, the thread of Spirit-anointed wisdom, and the thread of sound, practical advice—James Davis has woven a masterpiece! I will be a much better pastor for having read it. This book needs to be read by every evangelist, missionary, and pastor, because the Church needs spiritual leaders who understand the principles of evangelism and have a passion for evangelism! I would hope this manual will not stay on the shelf of your library, but will find its way into your spirit and mind. If it does, it could transform your ministry!

Tom Phillips—Author, President of International Students, Inc., Colorado Springs, Colorado

The Assemblies of God movement has historically been a focused evangelistic enterprise for the development of the kingdom of God. James Davis is a viable example of this tradition in practice, passion, and professionalism. I heartily endorse this book as a much-needed and long-awaited tool that will benefit and guide this evangelistic tradition into the future.

Del Tarr—President, Assemblies of God Theological Seminary, Springfield, Missouri

James Davis makes a strong but tender case for the Spirit-inspired truth that evangelists are called of God and placed in the Church (Eph. 4) because they are different. The Holy Spirit knows the diversity in the body of Christ that is essential for a healthy witnessing church. . . . Davis's treatise is especially poignant at the close of this millennium, as the role of the evangelist is again coming into biblical balance as revival fires again burn in all parts of the nation to join burgeoning growth of the Church worldwide.

THE PASTOR'S BEST FRIEND

The New Testament Evangelist

James O. Davis

GOSPEL PUBLISHING HOUSE
Springfield, Missouri
02-0783

©1997 by Gospel Publishing House, Springfield, Missouri 65802-1894. All rights reserved. No part of this book may be reproduced, stored in a retrieval system, or transmitted in any form or by any means—electronic, mechanical, photocopy, recording, or otherwise—without prior written permission of the copyright owner, except brief quotations used in connection with reviews in magazines or newspapers.

Library of Congress Cataloging-in-Publication Data

Davis, James O., 1961–
    The pastor's best friend: the New Testament evangelist / James O. Davis.
        p.   cm.
    Includes bibliographical references and index.
    ISBN 0-88243-783-6
    1. Evangelists. 2. Evangelists (Bible) 3. Assemblies of God-Clergy. 4. Pentecostal churches—Clergy.
I. Title.
BX8765.5.Z5D38   1997
269'.2—dc21   97-17775

Printed in the United States of America

This study is dedicated to my wife, Sheri Reneé
Davis, who taught me the value of sacrificial
love; to our late daughter, Jennifer Reneé
Davis, who taught me the value of a soul;
to evangelists worldwide, who taught
me the value of a biblical gift;
to Jesus Christ who taught me
the value of eternal life

And He gave some as apostles, and some as prophets, and some as evangelists, and some as pastors and teachers, for the equipping of the saints for the work of service, to the building up of the body of Christ; until we all attain to the unity of the faith, and of the knowledge of the Son of God, to a mature man, to the measure of the stature which belongs to the fulness of Christ.

Ephesians 4:11–13
New American Standard Bible

Contents

Foreword

Evangelism flows out of the heart of God. It is the announcement that salvation has come—the amazing declaration that the Lord of the universe has intervened in human history and through the mighty conquest of Jesus Christ, made a way whereby "whosoever believes on Him shall not perish, but have everlasting life."

Making this fact known is the business of the Church. Evangelism is not the only expression of Church ministry, of course. But it is the most crucial, for it brings the Church into existence and makes possible all other activities of the redeemed fellowship.

Every member of the Church shares in the work, but some persons, by virtue of a special endowment of the Spirit, are gifted evangelists. These men and women fulfill a vital role in the mission for the Church, both in proclaiming the gospel to the lost and equipping believers for the evangelistic task.

Strangely, though, very little has been written specifically with these gifted servants in mind. This book speaks to that need. It addresses issues which concern particularly the calling for full-time preaching evangelists.

The author, himself a distinguished traveling evangelist, knows what this ministry involves. For years, he has ministered across the length and breadth of the Church. In addition, as the National Evangelists Representative for the Assemblies of God in Springfield, Missouri, he has worked closely with numerous other evangelists. No one by experience and training is better qualified to prepare a practical evangelism book for the Pentecostal Church.

Certainly the strategic place of the itinerant evangelist deserves more attention in contemporary Church life. Believing that the wise council in these pages will do much to bring repute and effectiveness to this God given ministry, I joyfully commend it to you.

—DR. ROBERT E. COLEMAN
Director of the School of World Mission and Evangelism
Author of The Master Plan of Evangelism

Acknowledgments

In less than one week's time in 1997, more souls will be saved than in the entire year of 1900. More souls will be saved this year than in most of the entire twentieth century. It is estimated that by the year 2000, more than one million souls will be saved every week. There is a mighty wave of evangelism coming to every continent in the next century, if Jesus Christ tarries His return. This will be the result of a concerted effort at world evangelization.

The more Christians synergize together, the more they can evangelize together for the cause of Christ. I have seen this truth in action around the world. This book is the product of "principalized" synergy among family members, personnel at the headquarters of the Assemblies of God, and several evangelistic peers.

A special heartfelt thanks to Jackie Chrisner and Glen Ellard, who served as senior editors throughout this entire project; to Jean Lawson, for overseeing the project; to Diane Fulks for editing and compiling the Scripture index; to Kim Kelley for editing; to Chris Ortiz for cover design; to Leta

Sapp, for text design and layout; to Randy Jumper who provided the subject index; and to Jeff Fulks, who produced many of the project's graphs and charts. The statistical research would not have been possible without the aid of Sherri Doty and her research team.

I wish to thank my parents, James W. and Juanita Davis, and my grandmother, Clyde Davis, for sacrificial support and encouragement throughout my life. There is no doubt this project was first born when I answered the call of God on my life as a teenager. I am thankful for their consistent encouragement to answer the call to be an evangelist. I know this is my "patent" in life.

I want to also acknowledge the loving, parental kindnesses of my wife's parents, Evan O. and Marjorie Paul. They believed in me as an evangelist when few people knew of me in those early years. Evan helped to edit all of my research papers on both the master's and the doctoral levels.

The "unseen heart" of this evangelist is my precious wife, Sheri Reneé Davis. Sheri has given untiringly of herself for the purpose of world evangelization. This project for birthing, building, and broadening full-time evangelistic preaching ministries in local churches would never have come into fruition without her love, confidence, and dedication. She has edited my writings for fifteen years, traveled in ministry with me across America and around the world, walked through the death of our child, stayed up later than was healthy, and believed we together could make a difference in this world.

Truly, everybody is a somebody in the body of Christ!

Introduction

Have our evangelism goals in the Pentecostal church become root-bound, like redwood trees stuffed into flowerpots? Is the Pentecostal church failing to reach its evangelism potential due to limited horizons? Is the Pentecostal church willing to develop up-to-date, creative approaches to evangelism? The life of the local Pentecostal church must center around the biblical orientation of winning the lost. The cutting edge of Pentecostalism is evangelism. When the heartbeat of evangelism slows or dies in the Church or in a denomination, there will be more denominational buildup and less soul-winning movements. If the Pentecostal church does not continue to grow and go, then this Spirit-filled church will dry and die. In other words, if the Pentecostal church does not evangelize, it will fossilize! Evangelism and Pentecostalism are inseparable for the life of the church.

It will become obvious in this book that the ministry of the evangelist is crucial for continued vitality in the Pentecostal church. The gift of the evangelist is just as valid today as it was in the early decades of the New Testament

Church. God has called the entire Church to evangelism and has chosen particular people to be the gift of the evangelist to the body of Christ. Yet there is a great misunderstanding in the Pentecostal church today among the laity and leadership as to the identification and instrumentation of an evangelist. Many pastors and church leaders do not seem to understand the importance of the term *evangelist* in the New Testament or the divine distinctives of the evangelistic ministry.

In my opinion, the evangelist is to be the pastor's best friend in evangelism. Just like the shepherd needs the sheepdog to assist in leading and protecting the sheep, the pastor needs the evangelist to assist in leading and protecting the local church. Just like the shepherd and sheepdog work together, the pastor and the evangelist are to work together in evangelism.

As the Pentecostal church enters the twenty-first century, new maps for uncharted lands will be required to traverse the highly technological landscape of a global community. Evangelists and pastors will need to network to achieve exponential growth in a rapidly changing country. As pastors read this volume, they will discover new, unknown roads into the life and ministry of the evangelist.

For the first time, a volume is now available for pastors and evangelists to use together as a tool for excellence in evangelism. Of course, some chapters are tailored to fit the dimensions of a full-time, traveling evangelistic ministry. Yet I believe the pastor will deeply appreciate portions of all of the following chapters and will be able to apply first-century principles to a twenty-first-century Church. As a result of reading this book, I hope that pastors will have a working knowledge of how to

- align the local church with the New Testament laws for effective evangelism,
- recognize and utilize the New Testament evangelist,
- pray with power,
- develop evangelistic leadership in the local church,
- prioritize evangelistic ministry,
- prepare for a local church crusade,
- lead people into the baptism in the Holy Spirit,
- develop and deliver evangelistic messages.

If you are an evangelist, I trust that the contemporary research within these pages will prepare you adequately for the challenges of the twenty-first century. Just as an airplane must have a direction before departure, so must evangelists have a biblical compass before they can set their coordinates for effective ministry. Function follows foundation. By studying and applying this step-by-step model, evangelists will be able to design and direct their evangelistic preaching ministry on proven principles of effective evangelism.

The first-century evangelist is our biblical example for incorporating the ministry of the twenty-first-century evangelist in the life of the local church. Since most evangelists conduct weekly church crusades during their tenure on the field, the local church is also a primary focus of this manual. The gift of the evangelist, "functioning" in the local church for the purpose of evangelism, will serve as our parameters.

It would be high folly to think there is just one way to

birth and build a strong, vibrant, evangelistic preaching ministry in the Pentecostal church today. It would be naive to think that one volume alone will completely rectify all of the ills of the ministry of the evangelist. It would be arrogant to think that my teaching and techniques relating to the ministry of the evangelist are more resourceful and relevant than those of any other respectable evangelist. This book for evangelists and pastors represents the first step to removing the tarnish from a very precious gift in the Pentecostal church and will serve as a resource tool for twenty-first-century evangelism.

This research sets forth the steps for birthing (1 to 5 years; chapters 1 through 5), building (6 to 10 years; chapters 6 through 10), and broadening (more than 10 years; chapters 11 and 13) an effective evangelistic preaching ministry—culturally-relevant, Bible-based, and Pentecostal—in the Church. It is divided into chapters based on the past of the evangelist, the principles of evangelism, the purpose of the evangelist, the pictures of the evangelist, the person of evangelism, the prayer life of the evangelist, the phases of the evangelist, the priorities of the evangelist, the pastor and the evangelist, the practics of the evangelist, the preparations for evangelism, the Pentecostal Baptism and the evangelist, and the preaching of the evangelist.

1

The Past of the Evangelist

On January 1, 1901, the Pentecostal movement began in Topeka, Kansas. At the close of the twentieth century, Pentecostalism has become the strongest evangelistic force in the world. Evangelists have been greatly responsible for establishing the solid foundation and for spreading Pentecostalism globally. This brief historical overview will further crystallize the functioning role of the itinerant evangelist in the body of Christ. The dual tracks of evangelism and equipping will be seen repeatedly in the stories of these key twentieth-century evangelists.

There were many effective evangelists in the 1920s and 1930s whose ministries resulted in the enormous growth of local Pentecostal churches in the United States. These were the formative years of the Pentecostal church in the United States. Evangelists preached in storefront buildings, garages, skating rinks, brush arbors, tents, on street corners, and in civic centers. Their messages emphasized salvation through Christ, the baptism in the Holy Spirit (a subsequent work after salvation with the initial physical evidence of "speaking in other tongues"), physical healing, and the Second Coming of Jesus Christ. Miracles did follow these messengers.

Aimee Semple McPherson (a member of the Assemblies of God from 1919–1922) traveled from city to city for the "real establishment of strong Assemblies." Struggling home missions churches "were transformed overnight into thriving churches" (Menzies, 170). Innumerable churches became a part of the Assemblies of God during her citywide campaigns (Brumback, 271). Gigantic crowds attended these campaigns, and the Pentecostal message was expanded in America. She is the founder of the International Church of the Foursquare Gospel.

Maria Woodworth-Etter, who had a grandmotherly appearance, saw "countless Assemblies spring up in communities across the nation." She "exercised tremendous spiritual authority over sin, disease, and demons" (Brumback, 271).

Though he was born in England, Smith Wigglesworth, known as the "Apostle of Faith," came repeatedly to America in the 1920s. "No other person exerted more influence over the Assemblies of God with regard to faith for supernatural confirmation of the Word than this one-time illiterate English plumber." His paperback book *Ever Increasing Faith* has sold to date more than a half million copies.

Although nearly fifty years have passed since Wigglesworth's death, "few within the Pentecostal/charismatic ranks today would fail to recognize his name and know something of the exploits of his ministry" (Dorries, *Wigglesworth,* part 1, 4). For more than forty years, he conducted a worldwide ministry of preaching, teaching, and miraculous healings. The miracles in this man's ministry "represent a legacy of the supernatural that remains unparalleled in our century" (Dorries, *Wigglesworth,* part 1, 4).

His ministry began with the Bowland Street Mission. He and his wife, Polly, worked together for Christ in Bradford, England. For twenty-five years, Polly filled the preaching role, due to her husband's lack of confidence before people. Suddenly their street mission became a "haven for the people of Bradford to receive the ministry of healing" (Dorries, *Wigglesworth,* part 1, 7). It is interesting to note that before Wigglesworth was baptized in the Holy Spirit, miracles were already a part of his ministry. Through a series of events, he was finally baptized in the Holy Spirit in Sunderland, England. When he returned home to the street mission, all anxiety of preaching before people was gone. He now had "a boldness and fluency with language" (Dorries, *Wigglesworth,* part 1, 7–8, 32).

Miracles were a part of Wigglesworth's ministry before Baptism.

The trademark of Wigglesworth's ministry became the ability to lead others into the baptism of the Holy Spirit and to pray for the sick and see them recover. He desired "to awaken believers from their lethargy and proclaim to them that a life of victory is waiting for them through the glorious baptism in the Spirit" (Dorries, *Wigglesworth*, part 2, 22). His role model was Jesus Christ. Even though miracles did accompany Wigglesworth's ministry, "he learned through suffering and brokenness of the absolute futility of trusting in his natural, human capacities" (Dorries, *Wigglesworth*, part 2, 29).

Plotts epitomizes the pioneer spirit of a true Pentecostal evangelist.

In 1933–34, Morris Plotts preached evangelistic crusades in south central Iowa. In New Sharon, fifty miles southeast of Des Moines, Iowa, hundreds poured into his meetings. Some of the people drove more than one hundred miles to attend the special crusades. A large nucleus of people was saved and baptized in a nearby river. This was only the beginning of what God had planned for Morris Plotts's life.

The character of the New Sharon community was changed through this evangelistic crusade. Every aspect of this city was touched by God (Warner, *Pioneering,* 10), the results being reported in the *Des Moines Register.*

While Evangelist Plotts was still conducting crusades in New Sharon, he would frequently preach the gospel in nearby towns as well. On one occasion, he tried to proclaim the Pentecostal message in Searsboro (twelve miles from New Sharon), but residents threw eggs at him.

Over the years, Evangelist Plotts became burdened for world evangelization, particularly East Africa. He is remembered for his evangelistic zeal, pioneer spirit, and missionary vision. As an evangelist in the United States and Africa, against all odds, Plotts pioneered scores of churches. He epitomizes the pioneer spirit of a true Pentecostal evangelist.

Carl Barnes from Hays, Kansas, was ordained by the Oklahoma District Council in 1933. He was widely sought after to conduct revival campaigns and camp meetings. His crusades normally averaged between two and four weeks. Occasionally, he would leave the evangelistic field and pastor for a season. The churches he pastored experienced rapid growth. One example was Glad Tidings in Springfield, Missouri. Between May 1936 and April 1939, the church grew from forty to nearly five hundred people (Gohr, *Barnes,* 6–9).

Bert Webb was born in Fayetteville, Arkansas, on March 3, 1906. In 1925, at nineteen, he began preaching the gospel. As an evangelist, he traveled and pioneered churches. "His pattern was simple: evangelize in a new area, begin a church, pastor for a while, turn it over to someone else, and move to another city" (Gohr, *Webb,* part 2, 16).

He spearheaded a revivalistic/evangelistic crusade in Memphis, Tennessee, in 1934 which lasted for five weeks. During the outreach, nearly one hundred were saved and many were baptized in the Holy Spirit. This was an important factor in the growth and strength of First Assembly of God in Memphis, Tennessee, which became one of the Assemblies of God's premiere churches in the South (Gohr, *Webb,* part 2, 18).

Later, Evangelist Webb became pastor of Central Assembly of God in Springfield, Missouri, in 1939 before becoming the Southern Missouri district superintendent in 1943 and an assistant general superintendent of the Assemblies of God in 1949. Five years after leaving the Assemblies of God headquarters in 1969, he pioneered another church. This church was in California, and Webb was sixty-eight years old (Gohr, *Webb,* part 2, 19–20).

Ethel Musick was a legendary church planter in Oklahoma and Texas in the 1920s. She began her ministry by traveling with a Sister Tomson in evangelistic meetings. Musick later set out on her own as a teenage evangelist. After she was married, her husband traveled with her, supporting her calling as an evangelist. The Musick family typified the lifestyle of evangelists in the beginnings of the Pentecostal church. The Musick children "had few roots, no permanent home, school was only hit and miss, and they missed the ordinary blessings most of us take for granted" (Warner, *Legend,* 3–5). The Musick family was mightily used by God to pioneer churches. For example, Ethel Musick established six new churches and built five new church buildings in just eighteen months (Warner, *Legend,* 4).

James Robert Ashcroft was raised in an evangelistic family.

J. Robert Ashcroft was raised in an evangelistic family. He attended between twenty-five and thirty schools during his formative years. The John J. Ashcroft family conducted evangelistic meetings anywhere and anytime. In 1924, they spearheaded a camp meeting in Maryland where a woman named Hattie Hammond was converted to Christ. Hammond later became well-known as an evangelist for her "Deeper Life" teachings (Gohr, *Ashcroft,* 19). As a teenager, J. Robert Ashcroft began to hold evangelistic crusades on his own (Gohr, *Ashcroft,* 19).

Over the years, Ashcroft served as an evangelist, a pastor, an educator, and an author. For forty-five years he provided gifted leadership in higher education in the Assemblies of God. He served as president of four Assemblies of God colleges. When there was a "break in his full-time ministry in education, Ashcroft ministered for awhile as an evangelist" (Gohr, *Ashcroft,* 22). In 1994, his son John C. Ashcroft was elected as one of Missouri's United States senators.

C. M. Ward was a radio evangelist on the national Assemblies of God radio program *Revivaltime* for twenty-five years (1953–1978). He never repeated one of his thirteen hundred sermons delivered on the radio to millions around the world. Before coming to *Revivaltime,* Ward served as an evangelist, a pastor, a teacher, and an editor. He "received more than fifty awards, including being named to the National Religious Broadcasters Hall of Fame in 1993" ("Veteran," 23). Thomas E. Trask, the general superintendent of the Assemblies of God, described Ward's radio sermons:

> Each week his messages challenged the audience's minds and quickened their spirits as he invited them to the "long, long altar"

to accept Christ as Savior. And untold thousands did. His talents were many. His influence and ministry will continue to impact lives until Jesus comes. He has been a gift to this Fellowship and will be greatly missed ("Veteran," 23).

C. M. Ward died July 12, 1996, in Modesto, California, at the age of eighty-seven.

Bernhard Johnson is a dynamic example of an "evangelist to a nation." Evangelist Johnson went to Brazil with his parents in 1940. Over the years, he traveled throughout America sharing his burden for Brazil and raising the required finances to conduct his evangelistic campaigns. He was the founder and president of Brazilian Extension School of Theology and founder of the Children of Brazil Outreach. Johnson conducted 225 citywide crusades in Brazil and recorded some 1.8 million converts to Christ (Johnson, *Shanding,* 9). While preaching a missions banquet he suffered a heart attack, dying a week later, February 16, 1995.

These early Assemblies of God evangelists had no fringe benefits, no stable salaries, no permanent homes, no fine hotels, no extra monies, and no retirement packages. They were ridiculed, persecuted, and even jailed for preaching the gospel. Although they could have found easier work in the kingdom of God than pioneering churches, they sacrificed to lay a solid foundation for the Pentecostal church. Space will not permit to tell of Alpheus Broadhead, Edward Sanders, John and Will Bostrom, Jimmy McClellan, Mildra Mara, J. L. Jones, Raymond T. Richey, Lilian Yeomans, Hattie Hammond, Charles Price, John Follete, and countless others. In the formative years, these dedicated men and women carved out the evangelistic road for the Pentecostal church. They provided creativity, exemplified tenacity, and role-modeled Pentecostal leadership. They evangelized the lost, established local churches, equipped the saints, and exalted Christ. There is no way to count the hundreds of Pentecostal churches pioneered through the gift of the evangelist and the number of people who were called into full-time ministry during these crusades.

The Pentecostal church desperately needs effective evangelists with the leadership capabilities for mobilizing local churches in evangelism. Pentecostal church history reminds us of the importance of reestablishing the biblical role of the New Testament evangelist.

Evangelism Exercises

1. If a chapter was written summarizing your evangelistic/pastoral ministry, how would you want it to read?

2. In the last year, have you read any biographies or autobiographies about or by evangelists? Consider making such books a part of your annual reading.

3. Do you keep a journal of your evangelistic journeys? A journal will become invaluable if you decide to write a book about your evangelistic ministry.

4. Whom do you consider to be the most influential evangelist today? Have you read any of his or her books, magazines, or articles? Plan to read, study, and apply such materials to your life and ministry.

2

The Principles of Evangelism

Who were some of the evangelists in the New Testament era? What were their aims and accomplishments? What are the biblical roles of the evangelist in the Pentecostal church today? Can the local church reach its full maturity in Christ without the gift of the evangelist functioning in its midst? Can the churched, much less the unchurched, describe the characteristics of a true New Testament evangelist? Do Pentecostal pastors correctly understand what an evangelist is to be and do in their local churches? Is the evangelist crucial to the completion of world evangelization? In this chapter, several biblical principles of New Testament evangelism are analyzed and applied specifically to the evangelist in the Pentecostal church.

To call oneself an evangelist doesn't validate one's ministry. It is commonly assumed in the Pentecostal church that if a minister is not a church pastor or staff member, a college professor, an overseas or stateside missionary, then this individual is an evangelist. This assumption has created a vagueness in the minds of pastors about who the true, biblical evangelist is today. Consequently, the uniqueness of the evangelistic calling has been watered down. Exegetical parallels between New Testament evangelists and contemporary evangelists are needed in order to rediscover the biblical function of the evangelist in the Pentecostal church.

For evangelists to understand their biblical role and for local pastors to utilize evangelists in local churches, both need to comprehend the theological principles (chapter 2), the purpose (chapter 3), the pictures (chapter 4), and the person (chapter 5) of the first-century evangelist. The first five chapters of this research (the birthing phase) lay the biblical foundation for the calling, cause, and commissioning of the twenty-first-century evangelist. The biblical must come before the practical. Every

Every venture in life must have a solid foundation, or it will crumble.

venture in life must have a solid foundation, or it will eventually crumble. The starting point for evangelists will determine their mission, methods, motives, and message.

What is the starting point for contemporary evangelists today? A sound theological base. C. E. Autrey states:

> Theology is to evangelism what the skeleton is to the body. Remove the skeleton and the body becomes a helpless and quivering jelly-like substance. By the means of the skeleton, the body can stand erect and move. The great systems of theological truth form the skeletons which enable our revealed religion to stand (Autrey, 16).

Thus, it is extremely important for evangelists to discover who they are to *be* in the Church before they begin to *do* through the Church the evangelism they were called to. We must be willing to discard our presuppositions of who an evangelist is to be and what an evangelist is to do.

What is the meaning of the term *evangelism*? The Lausanne Covenant of the International Congress of World Evangelism (1974) provides a comprehensive definition:

> To evangelize is to spread the good news that Jesus Christ died for our sins and was raised from the dead according to the Scriptures, and that as the reigning Lord, He now offers the forgiveness of sins and the liberating gift of the Spirit to all who repent and believe. Our Christian presence in the world is indispensable to evangelism, and so is that kind of dialogue whose purpose is to listen sensitively in order to understand.
>
> But evangelism itself is the proclamation of the historical, biblical Christ as Savior and Lord, with a view to persuading people to come to him personally and so be reconciled to God. In issuing the gospel invitation we have no liberty to conceal the cost of discipleship. Jesus still calls all who would follow him to deny themselves, take up the Cross, and identify themselves with His new community. The results of evangelism include obedience to Christ, incorporation into His church and responsible service in the world (Elwell, 382–83).

World evangelization is the supreme goal of the Church. "Evangelism is to bear witness to the gospel with soul aflame, and to teach and preach with the express purpose of making disciples of those who hear" (Autrey, 32).

Even though Christ has commissioned every Christian to participate in world evangelization (Matt. 28:18–20; Acts 1:8), Christ has called specific people to fulfill the "gift of the evangelist" in the Church. Evangelists have their unique role to fill in accomplishing world evangelization. Just prior to Paul's pericope on the Judgment Seat of Christ (1 Cor. 3:5–9), he writes:

> What then is Apollos? And what is Paul? Servants through whom you believed, even as the Lord gave *opportunity* to each one. I planted, Apollos watered, but God was causing the growth. So then neither the one who plants nor the one who waters is anything, but God who causes the growth. Now he who plants and he who waters are one; but each will receive his own reward according to his own labor. For we are God's fellow workers; you are God's field, God's building (1 Cor. 3:5–9).

In these few verses, the apostle Paul reveals profound principles about evangelism. These truths apply to all ministers, but in this instance they will be specifically applied to the pastor/evangelist teamwork. First, evangelists and pastors need to *remember that the result is in the soil* (v. 5). The soil is a person's heart. Anyone who has been in evangelism for an extended period of time knows God is the one who gives the opportunity for preaching the gospel. Just as God gave Apollos and Paul the opportunity to evangelize then, God has given ministers the privilege to sow the gospel today. God is the one who is saving people, not evangelists. Just as God had unique responsibilities for Apollos and Paul, He has specific opportunities for evangelists today. Yet, they must remember the real potential for salvation is in the hearts of people.

Second, evangelists and pastors need to *realize the responsibility is the sower's* (vv. 6–8). In essence, Paul says for a period of time he "planted" (*éphúteusa,* aorist tense) the seed, and Apollos "watered" (*épótisen,* aorist tense) the seed; but God is the one who "was causing the growth" (*eúxanen,* imperfect tense). Before the evangelist ever arrives at a church or city, God *is already working* in people's hearts. While the evangelist is preaching in a church or city, God is working within the hearts of the congregation (cf. Mark 16:20). After the evangelist is gone, God continues working in the hearts of the people. God is working before, during, and after the crusade. He is causing the growth. He deserves the credit for the results in the nightly services and in the entire tenure of one's evangelistic ministry.

God is working before, during, and after the crusade.

God's reward system is not based upon the number of conversions in an evangelist's or pastor's ministry. God does not reward results. The reason is because God is solely responsible for the growth and results. Nevertheless, God will reward His servants according to their faithful labor in the harvest field (1 Cor. 3:8). Someone has to plant the seed and another has to water it. God will reward each individual for the team effort of evangelism. Evangelists and pastors need to remain faithful regardless of the number of conversions. In the mind of God, effectiveness in evangelistic ministry is not always measured outwardly.

Third, evangelists and pastors must *recognize that regeneration is in the seed.* Even though the seed is not specifically mentioned in this pericope, it is clearly implied. What did Paul plant? What did Apollos water? What did God cause to grow? The answer is the seed.

What is the seed? The seed is the message. The power of God for regeneration (1 Pet. 1:23–25) is in the gospel (Rom. 1:18). The preacher is to sow the gospel seed regardless of the various conditions of the hearts of the people (Matt. 13:3–9; cf. Mark 4:1–20). He sows because he knows the possibility of a thirty, sixty, or hundredfold harvest. There is power in the gospel seed. When it takes root, a life is changed for the glory of God.

With these principles in mind, the local pastor must provide evangelistic leadership before a scheduled local church crusade. For the gift of the evangelist to be fully utilized, the pastor must prepare the soil of people's hearts for the gospel message. The preparation stage has to come before the preaching stage (see chapter 11).

The gospel message is often called the *kerygma*. The kerygma is summarized

> # The local pastor must provide evangelistic leadership before a scheduled local church crusade.

in the words of Paul: "Christ died for our sins according to the Scriptures . . . He was buried, and . . . He was raised on the third day according to the Scriptures" (1 Cor. 15:3–4). If evangelists or pastors preach a "different gospel," then the curse of God will be upon their ministries (Gal. 1:6–9). The everlasting (Rev. 14:6), gracious (Acts 20:24), glorious (2 Cor. 4:4) gospel of God (Rom. 1:1) brings people to Christ (1 Cor. 4:15) for the purpose of salvation (Eph. 1:13). This is the kind of gospel evangelists and pastors need to preach today. We have good news in a society filled with bad news. John Paul has inspirationally written:

> The gospel is a fact, therefore tell it simply. The gospel is a joyful fact, therefore, tell it cheerfully. The gospel is an entrusted fact, therefore, tell it faithfully. . . . The gospel is a fact of difficult comprehension to many, therefore, tell it with illustration. The gospel is a fact about a Person, therefore, preach Christ. CHRIST is the kernel of the theology of evangelism, so we preach Him crucified (Paul, 10–11).

Evangelism Exercises

1. What is the starting point for evangelism? Why?
2. What does *evangelism* mean? Write a summary.
3. What is the ultimate goal of the Church?
4. What are the three overarching principles of evangelism?
5. How can you apply these overarching principles of evangelism to your personal ministry? Think through the issues.

3

The Purpose of the Evangelist

The purpose of this research is not to paint a full picture of each ministry gift in Ephesians 4:11 but to portray the life and ministry of first-century evangelists in such a way that twenty-first century evangelists and pastors can build their roles and goals on biblical principles of evangelism. Therefore, the "apostle," "prophet," "pastor," and "teacher" will be highlighted only in conjunction with the ministry of the evangelist.

The fivefold ministry gifts not only are representative of distinct people and ministerial offices in the Church, but they also reveal five principles for effective ministry today. The apostle, prophet, evangelist, pastor, and teacher represent the principles of governing, guiding, gathering, guarding, and garnering, respectively. All of these principles are needed for equipping Christians for effective evangelism. (See Figure 1 on page 40.)

An *evangelist* (*eúaggelistēs*) is a person with a divine gift and sacred calling from Christ to proclaim, or announce, the good news of Christ. The person who serves as an evange-

FIVEFOLD PRINCIPLED MINISTRY

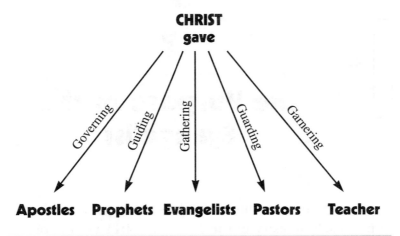

Figure 1. Functions of the fivefold principled ministers in the Church.

list is a "gospeler" (Drummond, 68). The evangelist's calling originally denoted both a function and an office. There was not much difference between an apostle and an evangelist since all apostles were evangelists. However, not all evangelists were apostles since a direct call by the Lord was necessary (Friedrich, 2:737). John Calvin believed there were times when God would raise up evangelists as substitutes for apostles (Armstrong, 33–34). In a real sense, "the apostles did not know when to stop being evangelists" (Brown, 69). Without the ministry of the true New Testament evangelist, the Church would die out (Bruce, 347). In all three New Testament passages (Acts 21:8; Eph. 4:11; 2 Tim. 4:5), the evangelist was subordinate to the apostles (Friedrich, 2:737).

"Evangelist" in Ephesians 4:11 seems to "denote an order of workers midway between apostles and prophets on the one hand, and pastors and teachers on the other" (Guthrie, 168). There has been much scholarly debate as to whether the ministry gifts consist of four or five separate entities. This debate is the result of the definite article being present before all the various leadership gifts except "teachers" (*toùs dè poiménas kai didaskálous*). The one definite article for both "pastors" and "teachers" indicates the "close association of functions between two types of ministers who operate within the local congregation" (Lincoln, 250). Even though there is an obvious association between "pastor" and "teacher," there are also distinctives in ministry (Acts 13:1; Rom. 12:7; 1 Cor. 12:28). This interpretation is paralleled in contemporary ministry.

As indicated above, sometimes these ministerial gifts (Eph. 4:11) did overlap. For example, Paul functioned not only as an apostle but also as a prophet, evangelist, pastor, and teacher. Christ used Paul in a fivefold gifting of itinerant evangelistic ministry. For this apostle, "the work of the ministry is of much greater importance than any hierarchy of officials" (Guthrie, 770).

Even though the term *eúaggelistēs* appears only three times, the evangelist had an effective and extensive ministry in the New Testament Church. This is indicated by the usage of the verb *eúaggelizō* ("to proclaim the good news") fifty-four times and the noun *eúaggélion* ("good news" or "gospel") seventy-six times. In Luke 20:1 and Acts 8:4, Jesus and the apostles were evangelists in preaching the gospel (MacArthur, 142–43).

Since the centrality of evangelism is derived biblically, theologically, practically, and logically from throughout the New Testament, it can further be deduced that the term *evangelist* is located in the center of the five gifts in Ephesians 4:11 because evangelism is naturally the central thrust of the Church. Regardless of the minister's work in the Church, evangelism is to be the main function. Evangelism is the heart of the Church. It seems reasonable to conclude that all of the fivefold ministry gifts focus on evangelism. As stated earlier, all apostles were evangelists, but not all evangelists were apostles. Moreover, all prophets were evangelists, but not all evangelists were prophets. All pastors were to do the "work of the evangelist" (2 Tim. 4:5), but not all evangelists were pastors. All teachers were to evangelize, but not all evangelists were full-time teachers. Just as the evangelist is the central gift of the fivefold ministry, evangelism is to be the central focus of the Church.

> **Regardless of the minister's work in the Church, evangelism is the main function.**

When evangelists are multigifted (apostle, prophet, pastor, teacher), there is greater diversity in evangelism. These leadership gifts are given by Christ to equip the Church for ministry. Figure 2 reveals the vitality of a multigifted evangelistic ministry. In post-Christian America, evangelists and pastors need to avail themselves of a multigifted ministry to reach people for Christ.

The twenty-first-century evangelist should have an evangelistic ministry as well as an equipping ministry. The evangelist must be able to appeal to the sinner regarding repentance and to the saint regarding revival. The position of the evangelist is critical to building a bridge between prophetic and pastoral ministries in the Church. The evangelist is a necessary link between repentance and revival.

The Pentecostal church today struggles to understand the biblical role of the evangelist in its ranks. Even New Testament commentators have difficulty in defining the purpose of the evangelist in the New Testament era. There is much written about the respective ministries of the apos-

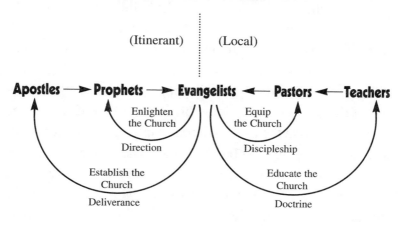

FIVEFOLD EVANGELISM

Figure 2. Purposes of evangelists in relationship to evangelism in the Church.

tles, prophets, pastors, and teachers, but not much in-depth research regarding evangelists. For example, some scholars suggest that evangelists are the equivalent of "traveling missionaries" or called only to spread the gospel in new places (Hendriksen, Lenski, and many others). Philip, the evangelist, is usually cited to substantiate this claim. However, even though Philip did travel to new areas to spread the gospel, Ephesians 4:11 focuses on the evangelist equipping the whole Church for evangelism. If evangelists are to be modern-day missionaries, then many denominations would have to reevaluate their entire missions programs. This will no doubt raise many questions about the roles and goals of contemporary evangelists in light of the New Testament.

In light of what has been written thus far, what is the purpose of the evangelist in the Church? The evangelist's purpose is clearly defined in the Ephesian letter. The aim of all ministry gifts in Ephesians 4:11 is for the equipping of God's people for the "work of service, to the building up of the body of Christ" (Eph. 4:12). The Greek term for "equipping" *(katartismòn)* means "to put right" or "to put in order" (Schippers, 3:349). In surgery it is applied to the setting of the broken bone (Wood, 11:58). "Equipping" denotes "the bringing of the saints to a condition of fitness for the discharge of their functions in the Body, without implying restoration from a disordered state" (Robinson, 182). The evangelist, along with the other four ministry gifts, is to set the local church in order, making each member fit for the work of ministry. In the case of the evangelist, this "work of service," or "ministry," is "equipping for evangelism." For the local church to be active in evangelism, the body of Christ must be spiritually healthy.

The Greek term for "building up" *(oikodomēn)* refers "to the act of building . . . to build on something, to build further" (Michel, 5:119–59). There is a fourfold equipping, or maturing, function for the evangelist in the church. Even though not specifically stated, these functions are easily applied to the pastor's leadership roles in the local church. For evangelists and pastors to function biblically, their message, motives, methods, and ministry must align with the Christ-given purposes outlined in Ephesians 4:13–16.

First, the evangelist is to help the Pentecostal church become mature in *stature.* The evangelist's ministry is to be active "until we all attain to the unity of the faith, and of the knowledge of the Son of God, to a mature man, to the measure of the stature which belongs to the fullness of Christ" (Eph. 4:13). This verse paints a picture of the Church maturing "into a perfect, full-grown man" *(eis ándra téleion).* "This perfection or

> **The evangelist, with the other four ministry gifts, is to set the local church in order.**

completeness is proportionate to the fullness of Christ himself" (Wood, 11:59). The whole body of Christ is viewed as one new man with one faith in the Son of God. "The faith" is the full message of the gospel. "The measure of the stature" (*métron hēlikías*) indicates a level of spiritual perfection found in the fullness of Christ. The body of Christ is seen as progressing toward its goal of perfection in the fullness of Christ. In short, as Christ inhabits our humanity, we are to display His deity.

A mature local church is an evangelistic church.

How can evangelists help the local church mature in spiritual stature? Evangelists should equip the body of Christ for its efforts at evangelism. A mature local church is an evangelistic church. When under the ministry of evangelists, each local church should be built up in the fullness of Christ to evangelize the lost in its community. When evangelists strive to equip the Pentecostal church, they should build up rather than tear down the local congregation. Is it possible that the evangelism efforts of the contemporary Church have declined in direct proportion to the decline of the credibility of evangelists serving the body of Christ today? Is it also possible that to recapture the spirit of evangelism for the twenty-first-century Church, it will have to utilize the gift of the evangelist correctly and evangelists will have to develop innovative, creative techniques for equipping the Pentecostal church for evangelism? Ephesians 4:13 indicates that the evangelist gift is required if saints are to reach full maturity in Christ.

Second, the evangelist can help the local church mature in *stability.* The apostle Paul writes, "We are no longer to be children, tossed here and there by waves, and carried about by every wind of doctrine, by the trickery of men, by craftiness in deceitful scheming" (Eph. 4:14). In verses 13 and 14 there is a purposeful contrast made between "a perfect full grown man" and "children." Instead of spiritual maturity, the picture is of "spiritual infantilism." The immature Christian is "swung around" by the wind and waves of "fashionable heterodoxy" (Wood, 11:59). "Instability is one definite sign of immaturity" (Harris, 8:139). The apostle Paul knew a lot about being tossed back and forth on the sea. Yet, it is far worse for Christians to be "whirled around by every gust of doctrine" (Hendriksen, 201). The concept that Paul teaches is not "physical infants in a boat who are helpless to manage it in waves and wind; but of physical men, who know nothing about managing boats, who are infants amid wind and waves" (Lenski, 539).

This dangerous preaching comes from "the trickery of men" and by their "craftiness in deceitful scheming." Those who preach this false doctrine are seen as willfully undermining the body of Christ. The term *trickery (kubeía,* from which we get the word "cube") was used in dice throwing. A cunning trickster would hold two sets of dice (Wood, 11:59) or loaded dice (MacArthur, 158) and would throw whichever set was best at the time. Such tricksters appeal to the immature Christian, who is often deceived by unethical tactics and persuasive words.

This is where the contemporary evangelist has often failed to mature the Pentecostal church. As I travel, pastors have shared their experiences in hosting some evangelists. The teaching and tactics of some evangelists today have caused the local church to fracture rather than to mature in sound doctrine. It has become fashionable for many saints to follow after these evangelists and their "signs." In essence, rather than signs following believers, believers are following signs!

Evangelists must take full responsibility for their message, methods, and motives in ministry. The itinerant minister must not participate in "scheming" *(methodeían)* to gain financially in the Church. Throughout their tenure on the evangelistic field, evangelists must make sure their evangelistic efforts write a biblically-sound, ethically-oriented "press release" for the Church and the general public to read. Once the evangelist leaves the local church, the pastor should be left with a more mature church than when the evangelist first came to minister.

Third, the evangelist can help the local church mature in *speech.* The apostle Paul continues, "Speaking the truth in love, we are to grow up in all aspects into Him, who is the head, even Christ" (Eph. 4:15). "Speaking the truth" *(alētheúontes)* means "truthing" or "doing the truth" (Wood, 11:59). A mature church does not tolerate error. Mature Christians recognize religious tricksters by comparing them to the truth. They correct the error of these religious charlatans by speaking the truth in love. "Truthing in love" keeps "every joint" (v. 16) limber and flexible in the midst of a changing culture. Someone has said, "Whatever is in the well of the heart comes out in the bucket of speech." When the heart of the body of Christ is filled with truth and love, Christians will lovingly speak out against all error in their society.

Since New Testament evangelists often travel from church to church, they have the Christ-given opportunity to build up the whole Church in the truth. The evangelist can also teach each local church how to distinguish truth from error and charlatans from evangelists. Moreover, evangelists should strive to equip local believers to share the gospel with love in their respective communities. Just as the pastor becomes the voice of truth in the local church, the itinerant evangelist becomes the voice of truth to the Church at large. "It has well been said that truth without love is brutality, but love without truth is hypocrisy" (Wiersbe, 2:38). The pastor should hold the evangelist accountable to the Word of God.

> **The evangelist should leave the pastor with a more mature church.**

Fourth, the evangelist can help the local church mature in *service.* Paul writes in Ephesians 4:6, "From whom the whole body, being fitted and held together by that which every joint supplies, according to the proper working of each individual part, causes the growth of the body for the building up of itself in love." The ultimate goal of an active, fivefold ministry is a "coordinated body with each member fulfilling his function" (Harris, 8:139). This maturing process depends on the truth that the various ministries in Ephesians 4:11 are interrelated. The whole body of Christ is being "fitted together" and "held together" by each separate "joint." The Greek term for "supplies" *(épichorēgías)* is derived from *choregos.* He "was the man who met the cost of staging a Greek play with its chorus" (Wood, 11:60). It is only when every aspect of the fivefold ministries are working together that the body of Christ receives the full support it needs to do the "work of service." The lifeblood of the body of Christ is love. Each member is to have a loving heart toward the other members of the body of Christ.

The fivefold ministries of the Pentecostal church are to function like an ensemble singing its various parts. They should produce a harmonic sound throughout the church. Moreover, each ministry joint should be limber, not stiff or limited by spiritual arthritis. When the gift of the evangelist is functioning properly in the church, the church will not be stiff toward the lost but limber and able to reach out to the unsaved. In the particular case of evangelists, they should fit together with the other ministry gifts. Each ministry gift should embrace the other for the dual purpose of equipping the church and evangelizing the lost. When the evangelist is biblically, spiritually, and creatively functioning in the contemporary Church, the whole body of Christ is more mature in stature, stability, speech, and service.

It should be apparent that there is a dual role for the evangelist in the Church. In the years ahead, the ecclesiastical discussions should not center around categorizing a person as an evangelist or a revivalist. Those with itinerant ministries should be encouraged to fulfill their New Testament position and purpose as evangelists. The evangelist should be involved in both a soul-winning and a strengthening ministry. The target of the message determines the teaching of the messenger. In the final analysis, however, the Pentecostal church in general and the local pastor in particular determines the kind of ministry the evangelist will have within the body of Christ. Evangelists can have a soul-winning ministry only when they are preaching in a soul-winning church or are given the opportunity to proclaim the gospel to unchurched people.

Evangelism Exercises

1. What five principles do the five ministry gifts portray?
2. What is the meaning of *evangelist?* Why is the gift of the evangelist in the center of the five ministry gifts?
3. How does the gift of the evangelist impact the other four ministry gifts?
4. What is the main purpose of the evangelist in the Church? What are the four other purposes that flow out of the main purpose?
5. How can you improve your evangelistic or pastoral ministry to fulfill the biblical purposes of the evangelist?

4

The Pictures of the Evangelist

The New Testament contains numerous itinerant preachers. John the Baptist, Jesus Christ, the Apostles, the Seventy, Philip, Paul, and others traveled proclaiming the gospel. Even though there are numerous examples of itinerant preachers in the New Testament, there are three distinct pictures that clarify what an evangelist is to do in the church. In the following pericopes, only the key words and phrases which further clarify the ministry of the evangelist will be highlighted. The aim of this research is not to provide the reader with a running commentary but to paint pictures on the canvas of the reader's mind as to who an evangelist is and what an evangelist is to do.

The Preacher-Evangelist (Luke 10:1–19)

Contemporary New Testament scholars (Ervin, Menzies, Marshall, Stronstad, and others) acknowledge that Luke portrayed his theology through his history. Thus, it is reasonable to conclude that as the author of Luke-Acts, he is giving the itinerant minister a theology of evangelism in Luke 10:1–19 and Acts 8.

The term *preacher-evangelist* or *proclaimer* denotes a person who is full-time in evangelism. In Luke 10:1–19, Jesus sent out the Seventy on a *dignified mission* (v. 1). The commissioning of the Seventy parallels the commissioning of the Twelve (Luke 9:1–6).

The Seventy were "sent ones" or "appointed ones" to work in the harvest field. They were sent in groups of two for accountability, protection, and fellowship. The Old Testament also required a double witness (Deut. 17:6; 19:15). They were ambassadors, given the authority of Christ to herald the message of their Lord. In New Testament times, ambassadors were sent to foreign lands to proclaim the message of their king.

Today, the evangelist is to preach and live in such a way as to reflect ambassadorship for Christ. The itinerant preacher is to be the bearer of good news from the King of all kings to this world. When the evangelist loses credibility as an ambassador, then an authoritative ministry of evangelism in the kingdom of God is forfeited.

> **Today, the evangelist is to live and preach in a way to reflect ambassadorship for Christ.**

The evangelist is not only on a dignified mission but also on a *difficult mission* (Luke 10:2–3). Harvesting is hard work. There is much work to be done and not enough laborers to get it done. Jesus already knew this. He did not tell them to pray for an easier job but for more laborers. "Pray" is the most important word in verses 2 and 3. Evangelists need to pray to the Lord of the harvest for more evangelists to be called into the harvest field.

Harvesting was also dangerous work. Jesus said the Seventy would be like lambs among wolves. These early itinerants faced the ravenous wiles of demonic opposition.

Furthermore, Luke describes itinerant ministers as being on a *disciplined mission* (Luke 10:4–8,10–16,20). There are at least two major areas of discipline for itinerants based upon the commissioning of the Seventy. First, they were to maintain the perspective of future judgment. There was to be an urgency about the work. The context of the commissioning of the Seventy is one of judgment to come. They were working in light of "that day" of dreadful judgment (v. 12; cf. 21:34; Matt. 7:22; 2 Thess. 1:10; 2 Tim. 1:12,18; 4:8). Evangelists were to understand the serious consequences for people who rejected the gospel or refused to listen to them. If the people did not accept them or their message, they were bringing down judgment upon themselves (Morris, 3:183). In essence, they were rejecting the gospel of redemption and would suffer the consequences. If a community or household did not receive the message of the evangelists, they were to shake the dust off their feet as they left town. This was a testimony of coming future judgment.

J. C. Ryle sums up the pungent truths of Jesus' teaching with the following:

> Those who reject the gospel, and remain impenitent and unbelieving, are not merely objects of pity and compassion, but deeply

guilty and blameworthy in God's sight. God called, but they refused. God spoke to them, but they would not regard. The condemnation of the unbelieving will be strictly just. Their blood will be upon their own heads. The Judge of the earth will do right (Ryle, 2:355).

The itinerant preacher is not to be despised by the churched or the unchurched. Evangelists (as well as all ministers) are ambassadors for Christ. Those who reject evangelists reject Christ. So long as evangelists are faithful to their calling, they are worthy of ministerial respect, financial support, and open doors of evangelism. It is a great sin for the saved or the unsaved to reject or neglect the "gospeler" of Christ.

> **The itinerant preacher is not to be despised by the churched or the unchurched.**

Furthermore, in relation to the disciplined life, evangelists are to be balanced in their priorities pertaining to ministry (see chapter 8). They are to be balanced in their physical priorities. Jesus did not want the Seventy to become burdened with extra supplies or baggage. They were to travel as swiftly as possible, preaching the gospel. They were not to be delayed by elaborate, cultural greetings. They were to trust the Lord of the harvest for lodging, food, and remuneration. They were not to "shop" for the best house to stay in while in a village, town, or city.

The evangelist in today's Pentecostal church should not be encumbered with high overhead expenses and worries of financial support. It is the evangelist's responsibility to behave and minister as an ambassador for the King. It is the responsibility of the local church to provide financial support for this minister's travels and ministry. Woe to the evangelist who places high financial demands on the local church. Woe to the local church that robs or takes advantage of an ambassador of Christ (Luke 10:16). If local pastors are negligent about utilizing the gift of the evangelist, then their congregations will fail to support evangelistic crusades. May the itinerant preacher and the pastor always remember that "where God guides in the harvest field, he always provides in the harvest field!"

The local church should support the itinerant minister financially.

As the Lord Jesus Christ continued His instructions to the Seventy, He told them they were on a *deliverance mission* (Luke 10:9,17–20). They were to heal the sick and announce that the kingdom of God was near to them. "Healing and the proclamation of the kingdom are linked together" (Liefeld, 8:938). When the Seventy returned from ministry, they were rejoicing because of their victories over Satan's kingdom. Jesus had sent them out as lambs, but they came back as lords! Then, Jesus explained the ambassador's "authority" as given by the King. In essence, he told them that as long as they stayed "under the authority of Jesus," they would be able to remain "over the power of Satan's kingdom."

Evangelists need to stay accountable to the Lord of the harvest as well as to their fellow laborers in the ministry. They should not isolate themselves from others in the harvest field. Also, evangelists must fight against pride and arrogance. They must remember that the greatest privilege is having their names written in heaven (Luke 10:20). There needs to be a well-balanced, evangelistic ministry in the Spirit-filled church today.

The Pioneer-Evangelist (Acts 8)

The New Testament evangelist also proclaimed the gospel in new areas. The apostle Paul and his party visited Philip, the evangelist, and his house (Acts 21:8). Philip was known as a pioneering evangelist. Why did Luke devote most of Acts 8 to Philip the evangelist? He wished to show that God used the gift of the evangelist (along with the Apostles) to preach the gospel to unreached people. While the Apostles were receiving reports of evangelism in Jerusalem, an evangelist was *leading the way* to reach a new ethnic group "in Samaria" with the gospel (Powell, 120). In Acts 8, Philip demonstrates many functions of New Testament, evangelistic leadership.

First, there were *supernatural wonders in his labors* (vv. 5b–8). These wonders occurred because of gospel preaching (v. 5b) followed by great power (vv. 6–7; Phillips, 148–49). The Samaritans gave heed to the preaching of

Christ (v. 6a) and were then healed by the power of God (vv. 6b–7). The power of God conquered diseases and demons. Even though Philip (cf. Stephen in Acts 6:8) was not "officially" an apostle, "signs" *(tà sēmeia),* or miracles, were a part of his ministry (v. 13). The term for "miracles" *(dunámeis)* was also used to describe the mighty works of Jesus (Luke 10:13; 19:37; Acts 2:22). Luke provides a "repeated emphasis in 8:7–8 on the 'many' who were healed and the 'much' joy that resulted (. . . *polloì* . . . *polloì* . . . *pollē)*" (Tannehill, 2:104). Scripture does not substantiate the claim that miracles were only attested by the Apostles (Stott, 148). Philip's evangelism produced joy throughout the city of Samaria (v. 8).

The Church should use the evangelist for the purpose of starting churches. Just as Philip was willing to go to the city of Samaria, the evangelist must be a willing participant in heralding the gospel anywhere. Evangelists should not only ask the Lord to help them communicate the gospel but also to confirm the gospel by curing the sick, casting out demons, and converting the lost. Just as Philip led the first-century Church into "new areas" of evangelism, Pentecostal evangelists need to lead the twenty-first-century Church into new, creative areas of soul-winning.

Second, we note Philip's *scriptural work for the Lord* (vv. 9–13). Simon Magus had been deceiving the Samaritans through sorcery (vv. 9–11); he claimed to be "the great power, namely God" (Haenchen, 303). Philip combated this deception with the Word of God (v. 12); he did not build his ministry on his personality but on the person of the Lord Jesus Christ. The people's faith did not rest on the miracles but on the message. Philip had a sound theology of evangelism. If individuals are won through sensationalism, it will take sensationalism to keep them.

Evangelists and pastors can be assured that when a true spiritual awakening occurs in a church or city, Satan will try to bring distractions and deception during the crusade. Satan has his counterfeits. Evangelists and pastors must make sure they do not become sidetracked in their ministries, but continue to proclaim Christ biblically through the power of the Holy Spirit.

> ## It will take sensationalism to keep those won through sensationalism.

Moreover, itinerant preachers always need to remember that true conversion is ultimately a personal matter for the listener of the gospel. For example, even though the basis of Philip's ministry was not the miracles, the basis of Simon Magus's belief was (cf. John 2:23–25). He was astonished at Philip's power. He continued to follow Philip to witness the miracles. Yet his heart was not right before God (Acts 8:21–23). Evangelists must constantly pray for keen insight into the lives of their listeners since they do not always have the opportunity to learn an individual's true character during a crusade.

Third, Philip's evangelistic ministry constituted a *submissive will toward leadership* (vv. 14–24). The reports of the Samaritan revival had spread to Jerusalem. After hearing of this revival, Peter and John were sent to Samaria to see this spiritual awakening firsthand (v. 14). Luke wanted the reader to understand that the Apostles supported the evangelism efforts in Samaria and were now coming to confirm and extend Philip's ministry (Longenecker, 9:358).

Evangelist Philip was a spiritual leader in the Samaritan crusade where the Holy Spirit was outpoured upon new converts. The Scripture states:

> When the apostles in Jerusalem heard that Samaria had received the word of God, they sent them Peter and John, who came down and prayed for them, that they might receive the Holy Spirit. For He had not yet fallen upon any of them; they had simply been baptized in the name of the Lord Jesus. Then they began laying their hands on them, and they were receiving the Holy Spirit (Acts 8:14–17).

Why did God delay the outpouring of the Holy Spirit upon the Samaritans until the Apostles laid their hands on them? In Acts 2:4 and 10:44, the Holy Spirit was given without the laying on of the Apostles' hands. The answer is found in this Samaritan narrative.

When Peter and John arrived, Philip slipped out of the limelight into the background. Immediately, Peter and John prayed that the new converts would be filled with the Spirit (vv. 15–16). Instantly the Spirit was poured out upon the Samaritan believers (v. 17). The Holy Spirit was given through the "laying on of the apostles' hands" in order to bring complete reconciliation between the Samaritans and the Jews. God was uniting the Samaritan church and the Jewish church in Jerusalem. The Samaritans were being "fully incorporated into the community of Jewish Christians who had received the Spirit at Pentecost" (Marshall, 157). God waited for the Apostles to arrive in the city of Samaria to bring an end to the division and racism that had existed between the Samaritans and the Jews for centuries (Wiersbe, 1:436). Furthermore, the evangelistic efforts in Samaria became a cooperative undertaking as Peter, John, and Philip worked together for the cause of Christ. Philip's evangelism efforts did not become an independent work. He initiated the outreach in Samaria, but Peter and John led the people into the Spirit-filled life. It was a team effort in evangelism.

When Simon Magus offered to buy the gift of the Holy Spirit (v. 18) so he could dispense it to others (v. 19), Philip allowed Peter to consult Simon (vv. 20–23). There is no indication that Philip was resentful toward the Apostles or that there was even a "partisan spirit in the early church" (Phillips, 1:154). The attitude and actions of Simon became a serious matter in this Samaritan crusade. Peter discerned the root of Simon's problem and urged him to repent

Working together for the cause of Christ became a cooperative undertaking.

before God. The term *simony*, "the buying and selling of church offices or privileges" (Wiersbe, 436), is derived from this story of Simon Magus.

In Acts 8:25, it is unclear whether Philip returned to Jerusalem with Peter and John. However, Peter and John evangelized other Samaritan villages as they returned to Jerusalem. The evangelism efforts begun by Philip in Samaria were carried on by the Apostles. There is no doubt John had been radically changed since his first visit with Jesus to Samaria. The first time he desired fire to come down from heaven and consume the Samaritans (Luke 9:53–54). God used an evangelist to set the stage to change an apostle's heart and for the building of a bridge between the Jews and the Samaritans!

God used an evangelist to set the stage to change an apostle's heart.

Philip's evangelistic crusade in Samaria included salvation, exorcism, healing, water baptism, Holy Spirit outpouring, Christ-centered preaching, reconciliation, camaraderie with the Apostles, spiritual discernment, and the exaltation of Christ. Philip, the evangelist, did not usurp apostolic authority. As stated previously, evangelists must stay under the authority of Christ. Also, evangelists must not usurp apostolic authority in the Church or pastoral authority in the local congregation. Evangelists must always remember their proper position within the body of Christ.

Moreover, the contemporary evangelist must be willing to move the Church forward in evangelism. Just as Philip went where no one else was willing to go, evangelists need to set an aggressive pace for evangelism and show the patterns for effectiveness. Evangelists must become "owners" of their "gift" before the Church will embrace it. The twenty-first-century evangelist would be biblically and spiritually wise to strive to include all the elements of Philip's Samaritan crusade.

Fourth, Philip had a *Spirit-led witness to the lost* (vv. 26–40). This pericope is extremely important in evangelism. The conversion of the Ethiopian eunuch marks the fulfillment of "You shall receive power when the Holy Spirit has come upon you; and you shall be My witnesses both in Jerusalem, and in all Judea and Samaria, and even to the remotest part of the earth" (Acts 1:8). Jerusalem, Judea, and Samaria had already been evangelized. "The remotest part of the earth" was fulfilled under Philip's evangelistic leadership. The sequence of Jerusalem, Judea, Samaria, and the end of the earth is geographical and implies the religious groups of the Jews, the Samaritans, and the Gentiles. It is extensively documented in ancient literature that the Ethiopians lived on the edge of the then-known world (Tannehill, 108–09). Luke probably means for the reader to conclude that the eunuch was a "God-fearing Gentile." Whether the Ethiopian eunuch was a proselyte or only a God-fearer, Philip furthered the gospel to the Gentiles (Bruce 186, 190).

Tannehill's remarks are outstanding regarding the ministry of Philip:

> In this scene Philip is richly endowed with the characteristics
> of prophet and preacher of the word previously attributed to the

apostles. He receives instructions from an angel and the Spirit (8:26,29), and when his task is complete, he is snatched away by the Spirit like the prophets Elijah and Ezekiel (cf. 1 Kings 18:12; 2 Kings 2:16; Ezek. 11:24). Philip can disclose the hidden references to Jesus the Messiah in Scripture (8:32–35), just as Peter does in his preaching after his mind was opened by the risen Lord (Luke 24:45). . . . . He is the initiator of the mission not only in Samaria but to the end of the earth (Tannehill, 1:108).

After the Samaritan crusade, the Lord directed Philip to go to Gaza (v. 26). Philip needed his *traveling* to be led by the Spirit in order for the Ethiopian eunuch (v. 27) to be evangelized. This man was reading from Isaiah (v. 28) when the Spirit spoke to Philip saying, "Go up and join this chariot" (v. 29). When Philip heard the eunuch reading the Scripture, he asked if he understood what he was reading (v. 30). Philip was then invited to ride in the chariot (v. 31) and to interpret the Scriptures (vv. 31–34).

After Philip baptized the Ethiopian eunuch in water, he was snatched away by the "Spirit of the Lord" to Azotus (vv. 39–40a). He continued "preaching the gospel to all the cities until he came to Caesarea" (v. 40b). The Holy Spirit directed the evangelistic ministry of Philip. Twenty years later, the apostle Paul found Philip in Caesarea. He was a family man with four daughters who were prophetesses. His family was serving Christ.

The point is that Philip was in the right place at the right time. God was able to use him both in public crusades and in personal encounters. Modern evangelists should desire to be led by the Spirit in their scheduling. Twenty-first-century evangelists must be willing to leave the large crowds in order to win one lost soul. More souls will be saved if evangelists are where God wants them to be. Often, the difference between a successful crusade and an unsuccessful crusade is the scheduling. Just as God put the evangelist and the eunuch together in a desert, God can place the evangelist in the right church at the right time for an effective crusade. Also, the Bible validates that Philip was Spirit-led in his *teachings* because he gave spiritual insight which resulted in the eunuch's conversion. Just as Philip had proclaimed Jesus Christ in Samaria, he "preached Jesus to the eunuch" (v. 35). Philip's exposition of Isaiah 53 found lodging in the eunuch's heart. Philip combined the Word with witnessing in order to reach the first Gentile for Christ.

In summary, Philip initiated the Samaritan outreach, and the Apostles confirmed the validity of his evangelism efforts. Philip began the Gentile mission. Later, Peter and the Jerusalem church accepted the Gentiles after the conversion of Cornelius (Tannehill, 110). There was much joy in the city of Samaria as well as with the eunuch, who "went on his way rejoicing" (v. 39). It should be apparent to the reader that the New Testament evangelist was not seen in a negative light or as a liability to the ongoing work of evangelism. The evangelist was respected by the church leaders. The evangelist was seen as being on the cutting edge of personal soul-winning, church pioneering, and crusade evangelism. Indeed, the evangelist sets the standard in ethics, excellence, and effectiveness in evangelism.

The Pastor-Evangelist (2 Tim. 4:1–8)

In the 1600s, John Bunyan was sentenced to jail for preaching the gospel. He wrote *Pilgrim's Progress* from the

Bedford Jail. *Pilgrim's Progress* is an allegory about a new convert named Pilgrim. The story begins when Pilgrim enters through a narrow gate and becomes a Christian. He is led to Interpreter's house to learn truths necessary for a successful spiritual journey. Pilgrim is first shown a portrait of a preacher.

John Bunyan describes the preacher as follows: "He has eyes that were lifted to heaven. He has the best of books in his hands. He has the law of truth written upon his lips. The world was behind his back. He has a posture as if pleading with men. A crown of gold did hang over his head." Pilgrim needed to first understand who the preacher was and what he was called to do.

Second Timothy 4:1–5 contains the graphic picture of the faithful pastor-evangelist. Like Bunyan, Paul wrote from a prison. The evangelism of any local church will be greatly affected by the preaching of the minister. To every pastor-evangelist in particular and every minister in general, 2 Timothy 4:1–5 reflects what a biblical preacher is to look like in the Pentecostal church.

The 'work of the evangelist': win the lost <u>and</u> equip the saints.

The apostle Paul commands Timothy, who is pastoring a metropolitan church in Ephesus, to "do the work of an evangelist" (*érgon poíeson eúaggelistou,* 2 Tim. 4:5c). It should now be apparent that the work of the evangelist includes both evangelizing the lost and equipping the saints. While Paul instructs us regarding the equipping of the saints, Philip illustrates the evangelization of sinners. It needs to be emphasized that the work of the evangelist needs to be operational inside and outside the local church. Even though every evangelist is not a pastor, every pastor should have an evangelistic ministry. Evangelism must be the main purpose of every local assembly.

In order to clarify the ministry of the pastor-evangelist further, one must study the context where "do the work of an evangelist" is found. Verse 5 is the climax to 2 Timothy 4:1–4 and the introduction to 2 Timothy 4:6–8.

In a broader context, the work of the evangelist for Timothy required him to evangelize even though he was not in a new and unreached city. Evangelism was to be a part of Timothy's message, methods, and ministry.

In the Greek text, the definite article does not precede "evangelist." Paul was not giving Timothy another job along with pastoring in Ephesus. He was saying that Timothy's ministry should be evangelistic in nature (Hendricksen, 312). The message of the pastor-evangelist is to articulate clearly the sinfulness of humanity and to direct individuals to Jesus Christ for salvation.

The pastor-evangelist is to perform the commands of his or her commission in light of Christ's return. The first command is to *preach conscientiously* (v. 1). The minister is to preach in view of God's presence (v. 1a). Paul was calling Timothy to appear in the courtroom of God's justice. The pastor-evangelist preaches God's Word before God himself.

Christ knows everything about every detail of every human being. Christ is watching everything the preacher and local church do.

The pastor-evangelist is to preach conscientiously *in view of God's pronouncement* (v. 1b–c). The apostle Paul dictates to the minister and the congregation the seriousness of the commission because of the One they serve and who will judge them.

The Christ who will judge all mankind will evaluate our ministry. (Our word *criteria* comes from the Greek word for "judge.") This judgment will begin at Christ's "appearing." Paul reminds us to always be preparing ourselves for the appearing of Christ.

The second command for the pastor-evangelist is to *preach continuously* (v. 2a–b). The evangelist and the pastor are to preach continuously *fulfilling the task* (v. 2a). The task is to "preach the Word . . ." "Preach" means "to herald or publicly announce a message." The pastor-evangelist is to guard the sacred content of the truth (1 Tim. 6:20; 2 Tim. 1:14), study the Word (2 Tim. 2:15), and then proclaim it.

Moreover, the pastor-evangelist is to preach continuously *figuring the time* (v. 2b). "Be ready" is a command and military term which means "to remain at one's post whatever the circumstances." "In season and out of season" indicates whether it is convenient or not, the pastor-evangelist is required to proclaim the truth. There is no closed season on evangelistic preaching.

The third command for the pastor-evangelist is to *preach comprehensively* (v. 2c–e). The minister is to preach with the *right tone* (v. 2c–d). Evangelistic preaching has both a negative and a positive side. The negative aspect involves "reproof" and "rebuke." "Reprove" is to biblically prove to someone that a particular act or teaching is sinful. "Rebuke" moves from the content of the teaching to the teacher or from the act of sin to the sinner. It convicts the sinner of sin. The pastor-evangelist discloses the sinfulness of sin and the sinfulness of the sinner.

The positive side of evangelistic preaching involves the exhortation or appeal.

Preach continuously— evangelistic preaching has no closed season.

An old rule for preaching is "To afflict the comfortable and comfort the afflicted." Conviction without a remedy adds to a person's burden.

Also, the pastor-evangelist is to preach comprehensively with the *right teaching* (v. 2e). The manner of the minister is "with great patience" and the method of the minister is "instruction."

The fourth command for the pastor-evangelist is to *preach correctly* (vv. 3–4). The itinerant as well as the local pastor is to preach correctly *before people lack the endurance for sound doctrine* (v. 3a). The minister must preach now because a time will come when people will not listen. "Time" means "a season or intervals." There are seasons when people will not want the truth. The faithful pastor-evangelist realizes that people can become unwilling to tolerate good, clean, healthy doctrine.

Furthermore, the minister is to preach correctly *when people lust for entertainment in accordance to their selfish desires* (vv. 3b–4). Paul paints the picture of a time when people will refuse to believe the truth. People have "itching ears." Sensationalism has replaced "sound doctrine." Evangelistic preaching does not tickle the ears, but burns them.

The fifth command for the pastor-evangelist is to *preach completely* (v. 5). The local pastor is to preach completely through *thoughtful evaluation* (v. 5a). "Be sober" means "self-controlled" and "stable." The preacher must face the issues with careful deliberation.

The pastor-evangelist is to preach through *tremendous endurance* (v. 5b). Evangelistic preaching is not a painless exercise. Diligence and determination are required to faithfully preach in our contemporary culture.

The local pastor is also to proclaim the truth through *tireless evangelism* (v. 5c). The work of the evangelist involves the preaching of soul-winning messages and the equipping of the saints for evangelism (Eph. 4:11). Ministry should have soul winning at its heart. When the heart of evangelism declines or dies in the church, the result will be a bureaucratic denomination rather than a soul-winning movement.

Last but not least, the pastor-evangelist is to preach completely through *total effort* (v. 5d). "Fulfill your ministry" includes all the duties named above. The pastor-evangelist proclaims the gospel with patience and careful instruction. He or she remains clearheaded in every situation, bearing the difficulties the evangelistic ministry brings. Regardless of our ministry gift in the Pentecostal church (apostle, prophet, evangelist, pastor, teacher), the central purpose is evangelism.

Long-term evangelists know when they are ministering in a soul-winning church pastored by an evangelistic pastor. It is obvious that greater preparation has been made for the crusade. Nightly attendance is higher. More visitors are present. More souls are saved. The team spirit between the evangelist and the pastor is focused more intently on the salvation of lost people. What would have happened if Philip and Timothy could have ministered together for the cause of Christ? What could happen today if evangelists would strive to be like Philip and pastors would strive to be like Timothy? Would our evangelism efforts be more effective?

What does it mean for the pastor to "do the work of an evangelist"? It means to specifically preach conscientiously, continuously, comprehensively, correctly, and completely.

Evangelism Exercises

1. What are the three main pictures of the New Testament evangelist? Summarize each one.
2. Which New Testament picture do you envision fulfilling in your ministry? Why?
3. Who are some past and present-day evangelists who have served or are serving as one of the types discussed in this chapter?
4. What are some adjustments you need to make in your personal ministry to fulfill the pictures of New Testament evangelists?

5

The Person of Evangelism

The number one debilitating fear of people is "having lived a meaningless life" (Jones, x). Do you know what your mission in life is? How can you know if you are making progress unless you have a purpose? The purpose is the compass and the progress is the coordinates for your life and ministry. In a sense, you have an "ambidextrous calling." You will have to remain faithful to the Word of God and still minister "in an ever-changing world" (Warren, 55).

Whether you are just beginning an evangelistic or pastoral ministry or have been on the evangelistic field or in the pastorate for some time, let me ask you one question: Why do you do what you do in the ministry? Is it simply to have a full calendar, money in the bank, or a national platform? Do you preach without purpose and minister without a mission? Let us never forget that the first and greatest evangelist of all time, Jesus Christ, could speak his mission in one clear, concise sentence: "I came that they might have life and might have it abundantly" (John 10:10). Even the early disciples knew what their mission from Christ was before they began their evangelistic ministry. Their mission was the Great Commission. Their goal was world evangelization. In evangelistic ministry you will either live your God-given mission, or you will live someone else's (Jones, xviii). You are either leading or being led. It is that simple.

Even though the following pages focus on the evangelistic calling, other ministerial callings (e.g., missionary's, pastor's, teacher's) can benefit greatly from the principles in this chapter.

This chapter will not teach you how to write a mission statement for an evangelistic ministry; yet, I encourage you to read books on the subject. This chapter will enlighten you as to the proper understanding of an evangelistic calling. This chapter serves as the bridge between the first-century evangelist and the twenty-first-century evangelist. With proper understanding of the previous chapters, you should be able to know by the end of this chapter if full-time evangelism is your calling.

How can you know that the life and ministry of the evangelist is your "God-given patent" for existence? There are many characteristics of an evangelistic calling (and they do overlap with other ministry gifts in the Church).

The Characteristics of an Evangelistic Calling

First, the evangelistic calling is *providential*. It has a sense of divine destiny about it. The call of the apostle Paul began before the creation of the world (Gal. 1:15). God knew Jeremiah before he was formed in the womb of his mother (Jer. 1:5). For evangelists to stay long-term on the field, they must know without doubt that God has called them. Otherwise, they will easily become frustrated with the stresses of itinerant ministry.

If evangelists do not know they are divinely called into full-time evangelism, they will eventually settle for "whining in evangelism" rather than "winning in evangelism." Evangelists cannot live with constant change (weekly travels, new hotels, different churches, etc.) unless there is a changeless core inside them. "The key to the ability to change is a changeless sense of who you are, what you are about and what you value" (Covey, 108). A divine sense of "who you are" will provide direction for "what you are to do" in evangelistic ministry. If money was not an issue and time did not matter, what would you like to do the rest of your life? Would you be willing to do it without charge?

Second, an evangelistic calling is *purposeful.* Abraham was called to be the "father of the faithful." Joseph was called to be a leader in Egypt during a time of famine. Moses was called to lead the Israelites out of Egyptian bondage. Joshua was called to lead his people into Canaan. The Old Testament prophets were called to proclaim the "Word of the Lord." Jesus was called to die for the sins of the world (John 3:16). Peter was called to be a fisher of men (Luke 5:10). Paul was called to preach the gospel to the Gentiles

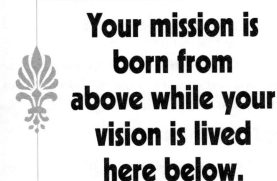

Your mission is born from above while your vision is lived here below.

(Acts 9:15; cf. Gal. 3:15–16). When Christ calls individuals to be evangelists, He has a unique purpose for them in the Church and in the world. Why does your evangelistic ministry exist? Until you are able to answer that question adequately, you will not be clear in your decision-making, what you should do and what you should not do, and direction, where you are going.

What are your roles and goals in evangelism? Your roles provide your direction and your goals determine your destiny. For example, you have a role as a Christian, but your goal is heaven. If you are in Bible college, then you have the role of a student, no doubt with a goal to graduate. You may have a role as a husband or wife, but your goal is to build a healthy marriage. These are three examples out of many roles and goals you may have for your life and ministry, and as can be seen from the Bible college example, roles and goals will change throughout life.

What is your vision and mission for ministry? Your vision will flow out of your mission. Your mission is born from above while your vision is lived here below. Vision is cultivated by (1) looking above you (what does God expect of you?), (2) looking within you (what do you feel?), (3) looking behind you (what have you learned?), (4) looking around you (what is happening to others?), (5) looking ahead of you (what is the big picture?), and (6) looking beside you (what resources are available to you?) (Maxwell, 145–48). If your vision and mission are fuzzy in your mind, your morale will be low. All great leaders know where they are going and are able to persuade others to follow them.

Third, an evangelistic calling is *personal*. The profound

insights of Novak (though written to the secular community) concerning "a calling" are remarkable:

> Each of us is as unique in our calling as we are in being made in the image of God. (It would take an infinite number of human beings, St. Thomas Aquinas once wrote, to mirror back the infinite facets of the Godhead. Each person reflects only a small—but beautiful—part of the whole.) (Novak, 34).

Numerous Old Testament prophets (Moses, Isaiah, Jeremiah, and others) and New Testament apostles (Peter and Paul) were personally called to proclaim the Word of God. The evangelistic call is not just a profession but a divine act of God.

God has not called you to live someone else's mission and ministry. A lot of ministers live "unlived" lives before God. Your true identity or self-worth before God is much greater than your present level of ministry. God does not call an evangelist or a pastor to develop a ministry on the "proven personality" of someone else but on proven eternal principles. Be yourself. Whether you serve on a large staff of an evangelistic association or in a local church, God still has a unique, personal call for your life. Vaclav Havel said, "The real test of a man is not when he plays the role that he wants for himself, but when he plays the role destiny has for him" (Buford, 23).

Fourth, an evangelistic call is also *practical.* "For a calling to be right, it must fit our abilities" (Novak, 34). Not everyone is psychologically able to travel for an extended number of years. One must have a changeless core in order to spiritually, physically, and emotionally adapt to a constantly changing environment. One must have a certain level of faith to believe God to provide financially on a weekly basis. It is recommended for someone interested in pursuing an evangelistic ministry to travel occasionally with a full-time evangelist to observe his or her lifestyle.

What are your gifts or talents? "One of the reasons many of us don't recognize our gifts as gifts is because they seem so natural to us" (Jones, 44). Why do you suppose God gave those gifts to you? There is a God-given purpose for the unique gifts in your life. It is our responsibility to recognize them, use them, and expect fair wages for the use of them in our service to God (Matt. 20:1–13; 25:29). Your gifts and talents will help you to determine whether you are called to ministry in general and evangelism in particular. Do not mystify God's calling on your life. It is practical.

Fifth, the evangelistic call is *powerful.* A divine call provides both the passion for the necessary creativity and the power for the renewed energies of the daily preaching grind. Novak states:

> Facing hard tasks necessarily exacts dread. Indeed, there are times when we wish we did not have to face every burden our calling imposes on us. Still, finding ourselves where we are and with the responsibilities we bear, we know it is our duty—part of what we were meant to do—to soldier on. . . . There is an odd satisfaction in bearing certain pains (Novak, 35).

The above observation easily applies to the lifestyle of the evangelist. If someone does not enjoy traveling, that individual is most likely not called to full-time itinerant ministry. If someone does not find renewed energy for the nightly preaching task, that individual needs to reconsider the evangelistic calling. If one does not have deep compassion for the unsaved or unchurched, that individual's evangelistic calling is to be questioned. If a man or woman does not find inner fulfillment or a sense of purpose in his or her evangelism efforts, then maybe their unique calling is in another area of ministry.

"If your mission holds no personal passion, it is not your path. Enthusiasm comes from the root words 'en' and 'theos'—which means 'in God.' What are you enthusiastic or 'in God' about?" (Jones, 49). Do people have to prime your emotional pump, or does your passion for your mission get you up when everything else in life is down? Even though purpose is the motivation behind dynamic evangelists, passion drives them to excellence when evangelizing the lost and equipping the saints.

Sixth, an evangelistic calling is *perplexing.* Even though the call of God is personal, sometimes it is hard for some people to discover it.

> Frequently, many false paths are taken before the satisfying path is at last uncovered. Experiments, painful setbacks, false hopes, discernment, prayer, and much patience are often required before the light goes on (Novak, 35).

Sometimes, several years of full-time evangelistic ministry are required before individuals know for certain that the evangelistic calling rests upon their lives. I know of numerous instances where ministers have left the pastorate for an itinerant ministry after they discovered their effectiveness was on the road. I also know of evangelists who have left the evangelistic field to become pastors after they realized their calling was moving to *a* church and not *the* Church. There are also those who know that their evangelistic calling is for a lifetime. They have served as the preacher-evangelist, the pioneer-evangelist, and the pastor-evangelist throughout their lives.

Are you seeking success or significance in evangelistic or pastoral ministry? There is a vast difference between these two concepts. Success is timely and dies when you die. Significance is timeless and lives on after you die. Soren Kierkegaard said, "The thing is to understand myself, to see what God really wishes me to do . . . to find the idea for which I can live and die" (Buford, 61). What is your all-encompassing goal in life? Is it to be an evangelist? Is it to be a pastor?

The Confirmation of an Evangelistic Calling

An evangelist is not only called by Christ to function in the Body but should receive confirmation by the church. The evangelistic calling not only requires inward affirmation but also outward confirmation. In the New Testament era, Philip was well-known and highly respected in his local church in Jerusalem. He was one of the original deacons chosen to serve the Greek widows (Acts 6). The local congregation also recognized that Philip was "filled with the Holy Spirit and wisdom" (Acts 6:3). It is important to note that before Philip was a leading evangelist among the Gentiles, he was recognized as a spiritual leader in his local church. The Apostles were also supportive of Philip, the evangelist (Acts 8:14). Philip was sent out from the Jerusalem church to become an itinerant evangelist during the New Testament era. Since Christ has given the evangelist to the Church, churches need to realize that this person is needed for the ongoing work of effective evangelism.

Has your local church recognized your evangelist gift? Have other church leaders confirmed your calling? Are there open doors of evangelistic opportunities before you? Do your family members and peers see the evangelist gift in your life? Is there an inner witness in your heart regarding full-time evangelism? Much soul-searching will help confirm an uncertain call.

The Continuation of an Evangelistic Calling

How can a Pentecostal evangelist continue to function in the church for years to come? Is there a secret for building a significant evangelistic ministry? What is one of the most important qualities for effective evangelism? In Ephesians 4:7, Paul writes, "To each one of us grace was given according to the measure of Christ's gift." Christ gives the evangelist "grace" to fulfill "the measure" of ministry. Each ministry gift in Ephesians 4:11 requires a certain level of grace to obtain the full measure of effective ministry. Christ provides not only the gift of the evangelist in the Church but also the grace to accomplish the intended task of evangelism.

The following chart (see page 81) is a compilation of New Testament exegeses regarding the principles, purposes, and pictures of an evangelist in the Church. It is intended to help evangelists achieve effectiveness and excellence in evangelism by providing both a compass and coordinates. The compass is designed to assist evangelists with their purpose and the coordinates with their progress. Questions under "the compass" will help ministers and Bible college students determine whether they are called to be evange-

EFFECTIVENESS IN EVANGELISM QUESTIONNAIRE

The Compass	The Coordinates

1. Has Christ called you to be an evangelist (Luke 10:1; Eph. 4:11)?
  a. Is it providential (Gal. 1:15)?
  b. Is it purposeful (Acts 9:15; Gal. 1:15–16; Eph. 4:12)?
  c. Is it personal (OT and NT)?
  d. Is it practical?
    (1) Can you travel often (Luke 10:4–8)?
    (2) Can you live with financial instability (Luke 4:4–8)?
    (3) Can you live without many material things (Luke 4:4–8)?
    (4) Are you a soul-winner (Acts 8:25)?
    (5) Are you capable of public speaking (Luke 10:10–11; Acts 8:12)?
    (6) Do you have the necessary talents?
  e. Is it powerful? Fulfilling?
  f. Is it perplexing?
2. Are you willing to evangelize different races (Acts 8)?
3. Has your home church recognized your spiritual leadership (Acts 8:3)?
4. Do you desire to equip the Church in evangelism (Eph. 4:12)?
5. Are you willing to fulfill the "the work of an evangelist" (2 Tim. 4:5)?
6. Are you willing to acquire the leadership skills necessary to lead the Church in evangelism (Acts 8; Eph. 4:11–16)?
	1. What is the main purpose of your ministry? Is it evangelism (Acts 8)? Is it equipping (Eph. 4:11–16)? Both?
	2. Do you exalt Christ in your preaching ministry (Acts 8:12; Eph. 4:12)?
	3. Are you accountable to your fellow ministers (Luke 10:18–19; Acts 8:13–24)?
	4. Are you submissive to authority (Luke 10:18–19)?
	5. Are you conducting yourself as the Lord's ambassador in ethics and evangelism (Luke 10:1)?
	6. Are you permitting sensationalism in your evangelism (Eph. 4:12)?
	7. Are you preaching false doctrine (Eph. 4:13–14)?
	8. Are you placing high financial demands on the local church (Luke 10:4–8)?
	9. Does the Lord confirm your ministry with signs following (Luke 10:9,17–19; Acts 5b–8)?
	10. Are you praying for the Lord to send more evangelists into the harvest field (Luke 10:2–3)?
	11. Are you a personal soul-winner (Acts 8:25–40)?
	12. If married with children, does your family serve Christ (Acts 21:8,9)?
	13. Do you have a "home church" (Acts 6)?
	14. Are you striving to "make disciples" (Matt. 28:18–20)?
	15. Is your ministry led by the Holy Spirit (Acts 8:26,29)?

Figure 3. Effectiveness in Evangelism questionnaire.

lists. Those questions under "the coordinates" will help keep evangelists on course for years to come.

Based upon my survey, pastors have great difficulty knowing who to invite to their church (see chapter 9). If pastors are going to utilize evangelists in the twenty-first century, they must know how to recognize them. If you are an evangelist, then ask yourself the following questions to further clarify your ministry. The pastoral checklist (see Figure 4, page 83) is designed to assist pastors in selecting evangelists for particular congregations. Every evangelist should ask the question: "Do I have the kind of ministry that pastors would consider both contemporary and New Testament?"

Evangelism Exercises

1. Are you called to be an evangelist in the Pentecostal church? Why? List many biblical reasons for knowing whether you are called to full-time evangelism. Check your compass.
2. If you are presently serving as an evangelist, is your ministry practicing the New Testament patterns? What are your coordinates? Are you on course?
3. Would pastors view your ministry as a New Testament evangelist? Why?
4. What areas of evangelism do you need to improve this year? Divide them according to "compass" and "coordinates."
5. If you are presently serving as a pastor, do you know the New Testament characteristics of an evangelist? Summarize them.

Pastor's Checklist for Selecting an Evangelist

1. What is the purpose of the upcoming ministry event (Ephesians 4:11–16)?
2. Will the evangelist fit the purposes of this crusade?
3. Is the evangelist known as a solid Bible preacher (Ephesians 4:12–13)?
4. Will the evangelist equip the saints for evangelizing the lost (Ephesians 4:11–16)?
5. Does the evangelist conduct himself or herself as a Christian ambassador for the Lord (Luke 10:1)?
6. Does the evangelist live by faith for his or her finances in the local church (Luke 10:4-8)?
7. Do supernatural signs follow the evangelist's message (Luke 10:9, 17–19)?
8. Is the evangelist accountable to fellow ministers (Acts 8:14–24)?
9. Does the evangelist refrain from engaging in sensationalism to attract crowds (Acts 8:9–12)?
10. Is the evangelist submissive to authority (Luke 10:18–19)?
11. Is the evangelist willing to go to a church when the timing is best for the local assembly?
12. Is the evangelist ethical in all areas of ministry?
13. Does the evangelist do the full "work of the evangelist" (2 Timothy 4:5)?
14. Does the evangelist focus on exalting the name of Jesus Christ (Acts 8:12)?
15. Is the evangelist a personal soul-winner (Acts 8:25–40)?

Figure 4. Pastor's checklist for selecting an evangelist.

6

The Prayer Life of the Evangelist

The priority of the evangelist's or pastor's prayer life will determine the power of his or her evangelism. When the biographies of evangelists God has used in the past are studied, the common denominator of prominence was their priority on prayer. Mighty men and women of God will have a consistent quiet time with God.

The first area of the evangelist's and pastor's ministry to be developed should not be the public life before crowds but the private life before God; however, many ministers do not have a deep prayer life with God. It will not be possible in this brief chapter to adequately cover the subject of prayer. For example, prayer for the sick will not be discussed though evangelists and pastors should believe God to answer such petitions.

The Reasons for an Effective Prayer Life

There are at least three reasons for developing a disciplined prayer life. First, the prayer life is for *spiritual conditioning*. The spiritual muscles of the evangelist and pastor grow as he or she "stretches" and "works" them out through supplication before God. The quality of the minister's quiet time will result in either spiritual strength or spiritual weakness. It is hypocritical to preach to people before first praying for them.

Second, the prayer life is for *spiritual cleansing.* Evangelistic travels are made up of dirty, muddy roads. Each day the soul of the preacher is

Mighty men and women of God will have a consistent quiet time with God.

soiled by the world. Non-Christian attitudes can creep into the heart. Sin can be committed even in the ministry. Thus, the prayer life becomes a time of spiritually washing the heart, mind, emotions, and will before God.

The more time the evangelist and pastor spend each day in prayer, the more adjustments will be made in attitudes and actions in ministry. The heart becomes pliable. The spirit becomes teachable. The will becomes responsive.

Third, the prayer life is for *spiritual conflict.* The evangelist and pastor are in a spiritual war for the souls of men and women. The itinerant minister faces demonic forces every day. When evangelists neglect the quiet time, they are weakening their guard before Satan and his kingdom.

The twenty-first-century minister faces the "tyranny of time." The most difficult thing to do is to prioritize prayer time every day. But evangelists and pastors must resolve to protect their quiet time with God regardless of the daily pressures of life and ministry.

The Rules for an Effective Prayer Life (James 5:16–18)

There is no way to overestimate the importance of prayer. Yet, many evangelists and pastors still underestimate its importance. Someone has said:

> When we depend upon organization we get what organization can do and that is something. When we depend upon education we get what education can do, and that is something. When we depend upon money we get what money can do, and that is something. When we depend upon what singing and preaching can do we get what singing and preaching can do, and that is something. When we depend upon prayer we get what God can do, and that is everything.

Evangelists need what only God can do in their lives and ministries.

THE CONFESSION EVANGELISTS MUST MAKE (V. 16)

Confession leads to consecration. Every great revival has been characterized by confession of sin before God and to one another.

The healing in James 5:16 specifically deals with the restoration of the soul and spirit of a Christian. Moreover, this kind of healing brings reconciliation and healing to unhappy Christians.

Revival also comes when confession replaces criticism. There is constant temptation in the ministry to criticize fellow ministers. The humble evangelist is careful to listen and understand before commenting about various issues and individuals in the church.

The circle of confession should follow the circle of sin. A *private sin* requires a private confession before God. A *personal sin* toward another person requires confession between you and that person. A *public sin* requires public confession. If a minister in particular or a layperson in general has sinned against the church, then public confession should be made.

THE COMMAND EVANGELISTS SHOULD MIND (V. 16)

James commands us to "pray one for another." Evangelists and pastors should pray for each other. It is harder for individuals to complain about you when you're praying for them. When was the last time you interceded before God on behalf of another? Ministers are not to be jealous of one another but are to pray daily for each other.

THE CONDITIONS EVANGELISTS SHOULD MEET (V. 16)

Our text states: "The effective prayer of a righteous man can accomplish much." Intensity is the context for this verse. The Greek term for "effective" *(énergouménē)* means "stretched-out prayer." The implication is not in length but in intensity. This is comparable to the athlete stretching for the finish line. Prayer will make you sweat. Prayer is hard work. Lukewarm prayer will not produce effective evangelism.

Ministers are to pray without ceasing (Luke 18:1; Matt. 7:7–11; 1 Thess. 5:15). In Luke 18:1, Jesus told His disciples "not to lose heart." The same Greek term for "effective" in James 5:16 is used for "lose heart." Moreover, Jesus constantly reminded His disciples never to cease praying. Those who search for God with all of their heart will find Him (Jer. 29:13).

The classic illustration of effective praying is Jesus' interceding in the Garden of Gethsemane. "Being in agony he was praying very fervently; and His sweat became like drops of blood, falling down upon the ground" (Luke 22:44). The Greek term for "very fervently" is the same word that is used in James 5:16 ("effective") and in Luke 18:1 ("lose heart"). Jesus was in agony; His soul was "stretched out" to the point that His sweat became like drops of blood. It is harder to pray to God than it is to preach the gospel. It harder to intercede before God than it is to inspire others to serve God. If ministers are going to have the mighty anointing of the Holy Spirit upon their message and ministry, they will have to agonize in prayer before God.

Leonard Ravenhill has summed up the issue well:

> No man is greater than his prayer life. The pastor who is not praying is playing; the people who are not praying are straying. . . . We have many organizers, but few agonizers; many players and payers, few pray-ers; many singers, few clingers; lots of pastors, few wrestlers; many fears, few tears; much fashion, little passion; many interferers, few intercessors; many writers, but few fighters. Failing here, we fail everywhere (Ravenhill, 23).

The devil is not disturbed by special singing, dynamic sermons, and crusade rallies that have not been bathed in prayer for the salvation of lost people. The devil laughs over much of the evangelism efforts in the Church.

The flesh does not want to pray. Prayer is spiritual warfare. Prayer is the "fight of faith." Intercession is more than merely mentioning memorized phrases in prayer. Ministers must pray when they feel like it and when they do not feel like it until they do feel like it.

Instead of being through praying, both evangelists and pastors need to pray through—touching the heart of a loving God.

THE CHARACTER EVANGELISTS SHOULD MANIFEST (VV. 16D–18)

The apostle James gives an illustration of powerful prayer. He moves from intensity to integrity. Elijah was a righteous man. Holy integrity before God produces power in the ministry. If evangelists and pastors want power with God, they will have to be pure before God. The Bible points out that: "the Lord is far from the wicked, but He hears the prayer of the righteous" (Prov. 15:29). Isaiah amplifies the thought: "Behold, the Lord's hand is not so short that it cannot save; neither is His ear so dull that it cannot hear. But your iniquities have made a separation between you and your God, and your sins have hidden His face from you, so that He does not hear" (59:1–2).

A sinful lifestyle will hinder the evangelist's and pastor's prayers from moving the heart of God.

Fasting combined with prayer further develops integrity in the life of the minister. Bill Bright identifies many benefits of fasting and prayer:

* It is a biblical way to truly humble oneself in the sight of God (Ps. 35:13; Ezra 8:21).
* It brings revelation by the Holy Spirit of a person's true spiritual condition, resulting in brokenness, repentance, and change.
* It is a crucial means for personal revival because it

brings the inner workings of the Holy Spirit into play in a most unusual, powerful way.

* It helps us better understand the Word of God by making it more meaningful, vital, and practical.
* It transforms prayer into a richer and more personal experience.
* It can result in dynamic personal revival—being controlled and led by the Spirit and regaining a strong sense of spiritual determination.
* It can restore the loss of one's first love for our Lord (Bright, 92–93).

The Results of Effective Prayer (James 4:1–10)

Every minister needs to learn to pray victoriously. Prayer can do anything God can do, and God can do anything. Evangelists and pastors need to link their lives with the God who can do anything. Jesus said, "Ask and it shall be given you" (Matt. 7:7), and James said, "You do not have because you do not ask" (Jas. 4:2).

Did you know that every failure in the Christian life can be traced to a prayer failure? Did you know every sin could have been prevented through prayer? Did you know that every need in life can be met through prayer? Each evangelist and pastor needs to learn how to pray victoriously.

THE PRESUMPTION OF UNOFFERED PRAYER (VV. 1–2)

God wants to bless ministers, but often the cares of full-time evangelism snuff out the life of prayer. Many are too busy to take their cares to the Lord. Preachers often trust more in their strategies than in their supplications. Pray first before trying to solve problems. When ministers bring their problems, pressures, and pains to God first, they can expect to receive the solutions God has for them.

Pride is the foundation of presumption. Pride leads to sin. John Bunyan said, "Prayer will make a man cease from sin and sin will make a man cease from prayer." Do you pray? Are you faithful in your prayer life?

THE PROBLEMS OF UNACCEPTABLE PRAYER (VV. 4:3–4)

There are times ministers offer prayers that God will not answer. James said, "You ask and do not receive, because you ask with wrong motives, so that you may spend it on your pleasures" (v. 3). The apostle James had in mind the motive behind prayer. If the evangelist is not careful, the motive behind some prayers will not be pleasing to God. If the desire is unbiblical, God cannot answer the prayer. Why do we pray? Is it for *selfish* reasons? Is it for ministerial gain? God will not sponsor selfishness or support sin.

Do we pray for *sinful* reasons? In verse 4, James states, "You adulteresses, do you not know that friendship with the world is hostility toward God? Therefore whoever wishes to be a friend of the world makes

> **Every failure in the Christian life can be traced to a prayer failure.**

himself an enemy of God." When a Christian falls in love with the pleasures and philosophies of the world, he or she is committing spiritual adultery. If evangelists or pastors are lured away by the world, their prayers will be unanswered. If they are friends with the world, they become the enemy of God.

THE PRINCIPLES OF UNDENIABLE PRAYER (VV. 5–10)

Do you want your prayers answered? There are five principles to undeniable prayers. The first principle is *sensitivity to the Spirit* (v. 5). Prayer is not possible without the functioning of the Holy Spirit in a life. The Holy Spirit has some strong desires and is very envious or jealous for our heart's total devotion to Christ. He wants all ministers to be completely dedicated to Christ. He does not want Jesus to merely have prominence in our hearts but to have preeminence. The Holy Spirit wants to lead evangelists in their prayer lives.

The second principle is *submission to the Father* (v. 6). Prayer is not a filibuster to force God to do something in evangelism. The itinerant minister must submit himself or herself to God. Jesus taught this in the Garden of Gethsemane. Do you want what God wants in your ministry and life? Or do you come to God with a hidden agenda or with your mind made up before you ever pray?

The third principle is *standing against the devil* (v. 7). Prayer is vital in the fight against the devil. There are demonic temptations in evangelism. Jesus told His disciples to watch and pray lest they give in to temptation (Matt. 26:41). Stand firm against the "schemes of the devil" (Eph. 6:11). Flee immorality (2 Tim. 2:22). Purify your thoughts (Phil. 4:7–8).

The fourth principle is *separation from the world* (v. 8).

Cleanse your hands (let go of the world); consecrate your hearts; concentrate your thoughts on God. Worldliness has no place in evangelism. Guard your testimony. Think carefully about your words before speaking them.

The fifth principle is *surrender to the Lord* (vv. 9–10). Remorse over sin leads to repentance of sin. When one strays from the Lord, one must repent through weeping and mourning before Him. When the evangelist or pastor exemplifies true repentance, the Lord will exalt him or her in due time. The apostle Peter wrote, "Humble yourselves, therefore, under the mighty hand of God, that He may exalt you at the proper time, casting all your anxiety upon Him, because He cares for you" (1 Pet. 5:6–7). This is a prayer promise from God. Learn to practice the prayer promises in the Word of God.

Here are other prayer promises:

- "If our heart does not condemn us, we have confidence before God; and whatever we ask we receive from Him, because we keep His commandments and do the things that are pleasing in His sight."—1 John 3:21–22

- "This is the confidence which we have before Him, that if we ask anything according to His will, He hears us. And if we know that He hears us in whatever we ask, we know that we have the requests which we have asked from Him."—1 John 5:14–15

- "If we confess our sins, He is faithful and righteous to forgive us our sins and to cleanse us from all unrighteousness." —1 John 1:9

- "Be anxious for nothing, but in everything by prayer and supplication with thanksgiving let your requests be made known to God."—Philippians 4:6

- "If you abide in Me, and My words abide in you, ask whatever you wish, and it shall be done for you."—John 15:7

The prayer promises in the Bible are there for the members of the body of Christ. Mark the prayer promises in your Bible. Memorize them. Study them. Apply them to your life and ministry.

How important is prayer to you? Does your prayer time reflect your answer? How important is prayer to God? E. M. Bounds writes:

> Nonpraying is lawlessness, discord, anarchy. Prayer, in the moral government of God, is as strong and far-reaching as the law of gravitation in the material world, and it is as necessary as gravitation to hold things in their proper sphere and in life (Bounds, 14).

Victorious prayer is answered prayer. Will you be a minister who will place praying before preaching? Do you realize the full significance of prayer? The praying prophet Bounds writes:

> Prayer fills man's emptiness with God's fullness. It fills man's poverty with God's riches. It puts away man's weakness with God's strength. It banishes man's littleness with God's greatness. . . . Men are never nearer heaven, nearer God, never more Godlike, never in deeper sympathy and truer partnership with Jesus Christ, than when praying.
>
> Prayer is not merely a question of duty, but of salvation. Are men saved who are not men of prayer? Is not the gift, the inclination, the habit of prayer, one of the elements or characteristics of salvation? Can it be possible to be in affinity with Jesus Christ and not be prayerful? Is it possible to have the Holy Spirit and not have the spirit of prayer? Can one have the new birth and not be born to prayer? . . . Can brotherly love be in the heart which is unschooled in prayer? (Bounds, 20).

Imagine what one evangelist or pastor can do through prayer and fasting combined with the preaching of the gospel. Martin Luther led the Protestant Reformation. John Knox said, "Give me Scotland or I die." John Bunyon wrote *Pilgrim's Progress* from the Bedford Jail. Jonathan Edwards sparked the flames of a Great Spiritual Awakening through his sermon "Sinners in the Hands of An Angry God." George Whitfield, Charles Wesley, D. L. Moody, Charles G. Finney, and Billy Graham have all fulfilled God's purpose for ministry during their respective generations. Will you fulfill the role of the evangelist in the twenty-first century?

Will you be known for your prayer life or your public life? Do you believe prayer is one of the greatest steps to birthing, building, and broadening a full-time evangelistic preaching ministry? This chapter serves only as a summary of the prayer life of the minister. Did you have a quiet time today?

Evangelism Exercises

1. How would you rate your prayer life on a scale from one to ten, with ten being the best? List several ways to improve your prayer life.
2. Do you have a plan to deepen your prayer life? Think of a prayer plan including Bible study and biographies of evangelists of the past.
3. Are you memorizing prayer promises?
4. Have you considered writing a prayer journal, noting answers to your prayers? For the next thirty days, write down your prayers and the dates your prayers are answered.

7

The Phases of the Evangelist

Once a person has settled the issue forever regarding the evangelistic or pastoral call of God upon his or her life, then that individual must prepare to become a leader in the Pentecostal church. If you are beginning an evangelistic or pastoral ministry, you must comprehend what true evangelistic leadership is about in the church. Instead of asking, "Why is my ministry not growing?" ask, "What makes a ministry grow?" An effective ministry will naturally grow.

God is not calling evangelists and pastors to be managers but leaders. There is a great difference between managers and leaders of evangelism. Warren Bennis notes:

*The manager administers; the leader innovates.
*The manager is a copy; the leader is an original.
*The manager maintains; the leader develops.
*The manager focuses on systems and structures; the
  leader focuses on people.
*The manager relies on control; the leader inspires trust.
*The manager has a short-range view; the leader has a
  long-range view.

*The manager asks how and when; the leader asks what and why.

*The manager has his eye on the bottom line; the leader has his eye on the horizon.

*The manager imitates; the leader originates.

*The manager accepts the status quo; the leader challenges and changes it.

*The manager is the classic good soldier; the leader is his own person.

*The manager does things right; the leader does the right things (Bennis, 45).

Why doesn't every evangelist have significant influence both in the church and country? Why is every evangelist not on the cutting edge? Years ago, I discovered that the answer is creative Pentecostal, Bible-based leadership in the church. "Creativity" involves imagination. "Pentecostal" consists of inspiration. "Bible-based" constitutes indoctrination. "Leadership" provides influence. All of these elements are necessary to be effective in equipping the saints and evangelizing the lost. The truths are applicable both in the local church and on the evangelistic field.

The Principles of Evangelistic Leadership

Leadership is not about position but people, not about rank but relationships, not about titles but transitions, not about information but influence. If an individual does not have followers, then he or she is not a leader. We are either leading or being led. This principle can easily be applied to evangelists and pastors in the twenty-first-century Church. Evangelists, as well as all the other ministry gifts in Ephesians 4:11–16, are to lead the Church in stature, stability, speech, and service (see chapter 2). If evangelists are not leading the Church in evangelism, then they are being led in evangelism by others. If pastors are not leading the local church in evangelism, then they are being led in evangelism by others. If this be the case, then they have forfeited their evangelistic leadership role to someone else in the body of Christ. In the evangelical church in general and the Pentecostal church in particular, the emphasis shifted gradually from a fivefold ministry gift to a twofold ministry gift (i.e., pastor and teacher). This is not necessarily the fault of the Pentecostal church or the evangelical church as a whole. Evangelists must decide to lead the Pentecostal church again in the twenty-first century. They must become owners of their gift and strive to improve their leadership skills.

For example, in Acts 8 Philip did not wait on the Apostles, but proceeded to provide evangelistic leadership to the Samaritans and Gentiles (see chapter 3). Even though it is the biblical responsibility of the local and national leadership of the Pentecostal church to recognize and utilize the gift of the evangelist in its ranks, individual evangelists must decide, like Philip, to be led by the Holy Spirit so they may in turn lead the church in evangelism. Evangelistic leadership is a long, treacherous jour-

Evangelists must own their gift, improve their leadership.

ney upward on the winding, hairpin-curved, rutted roads of decision making (what to do), discipline (when to do it), discernment (why do it), determination (who should do it), and development (how to do it) to the peak of long-lasting significance in the church. In many ways, evangelistic leadership is both a biblical and ecclesiastical odyssey with traveling routes to the undiscovered worlds of revival in the church and salvation of the lost.

John C. Maxwell observes:

> Everything rises and falls on leadership. . . . Most people have a desire to look for the exception instead of the desire to become exceptional. . . . The effectiveness of your work will never rise above your ability to lead and influence others. You cannot produce consistently on a level higher than your leadership. In other words, your leadership skills determine the level of your success—and the success of those who work around you (Maxwell, 2).

The Phases of Evangelistic Leadership

There are five levels of leadership in the church (Maxwell, 5–11). These five levels of leadership apply to all five ministry gifts in the church, but have been tailored to fit the twenty-first-century evangelist. It is important to note that the higher the level of evangelistic leadership, the greater the influence in the body of Christ. Evangelists and pastors need to know their level of leadership in order to increase their level of influence. For example, the level of influence of evangelists in the Pentecostal church has decreased in the latter part of the twentieth century. Thus, it is extremely crucial for evangelists to recognize the level they are on corporately and individually in the body of Christ and recommit themselves to developing evangelistic leadership skills for the twenty-first century.

The first level of the evangelistic leadership paradigm is the position phase. This phase involves the *evangelist's responsibilities in the church.* This is the doorway into evangelistic leadership. Men and women step through this door when they accept Christ's call to be full-time evangelists. Yet, people will not follow an evangelist very far on this level because of the lack of recognized authority in the church. It is possible to have been given authority by Christ to fulfill the evangelist's role in the church and still not be recognized as possessing that evangelistic authority. This is a sad scenario, but true. The first level of evangelistic leadership includes answering God's call (the private life), accountability to others (the public life), and aim in ministry (the purposeful life).

The next aspect of the position phase is accountability to peers. This is foundational for a faithful, fruitful, and lifetime evangelistic ministry. One must be accountable spiritually, morally, and financially. Know yourself. Keep a journal.

The last dimension of the position phase involves the aim of ministry. Within the first year of my evangelistic ministry, I developed a mission statement. If you do not know who you are and where you are going, then you will not accomplish much and will end up nowhere. The action steps necessary to mastering level one are as follows:

1. Know your New Testament, evangelistic calling thoroughly.
2. Research the historical work of the evangelist in the church.

3. Become the owner of your evangelistic gift.
4. Accept responsibility for your evangelistic ministry.
5. Strive for excellence without extravagance.
6. Give more than is expected of you.
7. Provide creative ideas for evangelism in the church.
8. Be proactive.
9. Take the long view instead of the short view.

The second level of evangelistic leadership is the permission phase. This level involves the *evangelist's relationships in the church*. The greater the deposits into people's emotional bank accounts, the greater the withdrawals can be in the future. Effective evangelistic ministry is made up of relationships with evangelists, pastors, both state and national church leadership, and laity. In the final analysis, "leadership is getting people to work for you when they are not obligated. . . . That will only happen when you move to the second level of leadership. People do not care how much you know until they know how much you care" (Maxwell, 7). Your evangelistic leadership and ministry will not grow nor expand by imposing regulations on the local church, telling them what to do and not to do as it relates to you. They will mature, however, by growing relationships with local pastors. Evangelists who fail to develop long-lasting pastoral relationships will experience a short-lived tenure on the field, and their leadership influence will not move to level three.

This research contains the findings from a mail survey conducted by Cutting Edge International, in conjunction with the National Evangelists Office at the Assemblies of

God headquarters in Springfield, Missouri. The survey was conducted between May and July 1996 with pastors of the leading 2,000 Assemblies of God churches (according to Sunday morning attendance) and the 850 Assemblies of God evangelists in the United States. The objectives of the study were (1) to determine the overall pastoral perception of specific topics relating to evangelists, (2) to determine the most important needs of evangelists, and (3) to establish the average number of years required to reach various levels of full-time evangelism. This survey represents the first concerted effort ever to begin a national discussion among evangelists and local pastors to achieve effective evangelism.

The two survey questionnaires were the product of in-depth interviews with a select group of full-time evangelists, leading pastors, and the national leaders of the Assemblies of God. Upon receipt of the completed surveys from the respondents, the statistician at the Assemblies of God headquarters tabulated the answers by computer. The results of this survey (see pages 109, 132) reveal the difficulties pastors have in finding the right evangelist and the difficulties evangelists have in maintaining a full preaching calendar and financial stability. Furthermore, with the present low credibility of the evangelist in both our culture and the church, many hard years are required to move from level two to level three. Evangelists living or "surviving" on level two usually initiate the invitation by contacting the pastor, have a half-filled calendar, experience financial instability, have insufficient health insurance, and know the frustration of many cancellations. The only way to move to the next level is through private resources (a solid devotional life, an expanding library, and growing through tapes and seminars), personal relationships, and public results. This is a continual process in evangelistic leadership. Ecclesiastes 10:10 declares: "If the ax is dull and he does not sharpen its edge, then he must exert more strength. Wisdom has the advantage of giving success." Take the time to sharpen the edge of your evangelism. Just because an evangelist moves to level three does not mean the dynamics of levels one and two cease to be necessary.

Do not try to skip level two. Even though level three is the growth stage, level two is the glue stage. The deeper the permission level in the church, the higher the production level. This principle is true in the family, the local church, and in the national arena of ideas for the twenty-first-century Pentecostal church. The action steps to master level two are as follows:

1. Love people unconditionally.
2. Make the pastor more successful.
3. Be a servant.
4. Seek "win-win" or no deal.
5. Be a people person.
6. Use wisdom with difficult people.
7. Make one close friend per year.
8. Turn old ministry into new ministry.
9. Get visible in the church.
10. Cultivate a winning attitude.
11. Develop your preaching skills.

The third level of evangelistic leadership is the production phase. This level involves the *evangelist's results in the church*. Evangelists who minister on this level regularly receive invitations from pastors, maintain a full calendar, experience financial stability, and have few cancellations. Their influence deepens in the church. They have a national ministry, a following of both laypeople and ministers because of what the evangelist has done for the entire church. There is momentum in the ministry.

Evangelists who live on this level are purpose driven. They understand that purpose determines priorities, priorities design programs, and programs dictate procedures. What they do on a weekly basis flows out of where they are going in ministry. They do not base their mission on the clock or the calendar but on the compass. They are not driven by dates and deadlines alone but by direction. The action steps to mastering level three are as follows:

1. Continue the process of levels one and two in both new and repeat churches.
2. Strive for significance instead of success.
3. Crystallize your mission statement and follow it.
4. Do high-production activities first (see chapter 8).
5. Be willing to take well-thought-out risks.
6. Communicate vision.
7. Develop an accountable team for purposeful results.
8. Be a change agent in the church.
9. Have a good sense of timing.
10. Personally know the key influencers in the church.
11. Develop your preaching skills.

The fourth level of evangelistic leadership is the "people development" phase. This level involves the *evangelist's reproduction in the church.* When evangelists operate on this level of ministry, they are frequently invited to return to the same local church and are mentoring and training future evangelistic leaders in the body of Christ. True leadership is not made of one's own power but of the empowerment of others. On this level, evangelists understand that their main responsibility is equipping others in evangelism. Few evangelists reach or desire this level of leadership. Most evangelists struggle so much with schedules and finances that they seldom see the bigger picture of evangelism. Evangelists must win the lost not only through nightly "additions" to Christ but also through the "multiplication" of more equipped evangelists.

Many evangelists are so consumed with looking at the bottom line that they fail to look at the horizon. I am convinced that the people development phase is the most fulfilling of all the previous phases of evangelistic leadership. Will you win the lost to Christ through addition by decisions for Christ or through multiplication by disciples for Christ?

Many renown leaders have said, "Success without a successor is failure" (Burford, Maxwell, Waitley, and others). This is where followership leads to mentorship. At this level, laypeople and ministers follow the evangelist because of what he or she has done for them personally. Many years of growing evangelistic leaders are required before an evangelist reaches this level in the body of Christ. However, "the more people you lead the more leaders you need" (Maxwell, 13). Evangelistic leaders need "sounding boards" and "springboards" (Waitley, 41). Sounding boards are people who provide consultation, listening to ideas, giving feedback, sharing good judgment, and springboards are key leaders who provide contacts. The action steps to mastering level four are as follows:

1. Continue the process of levels one through three in new and repeat churches and with new evangelists.
2. Be a role model.
3. Synergize with a core of leaders who complement your vision and mission.
4. Expose key pastors and evangelists to personal growth opportunities.
5. Continue to attract high achievers to your common goal.
6. Think creatively, "outside the box" (see Vance and Deacon), for maximum effectiveness.
7. Develop your preaching skills.

The fifth level of evangelistic leadership is the personhood phase. This level involves the *evangelist's respect in the church.* Very few obtain this level of leadership throughout most of their evangelistic ministry. This is not just some goal to be sought but is a providential, God-ordained place of leadership. This five-level paradigm is not to suggest that dynamic leadership can be boiled down to a formula for success. Our evangelistic motives and ethics must be impeccable before Christ and His Church.

However, the evangelist who functions on level five has definite influence in the world and is bigger than life itself. This level of leadership happens as a result of the constant private victories that lead to the public victories. This final level of leadership does not occur in a person's life or ministry merely by appointments or elections but through an entire lifetime of recycling levels one through four in the entire body of Christ. Each level of evangelistic leadership stands upon the previous one. None of the previous levels can be neglected without a ministry meltdown before the biblical and ecclesiastical odyssey of evangelism is completed. Evangelists ministering on this final level have spent years mentoring and molding evangelists and pastors in the church.

Church history records many evangelists who served God faithfully to the end. They fulfilled God's purpose for their lives and ministry. They

Each leadership level stands upon the previous one.

may not have viewed their ministry through this five-level lens, yet they were bigger than life then and left examples of true evangelistic leadership for us today. With the rising tide of every spiritual awakening in history, God raises up evangelists to lead the Church in evangelism. The last three centuries contain illustrations of this. In the eighteenth century, God thrust George Whitfield and John Wesley to the forefront. In the nineteenth century, Charles G. Finney, D. L. Moody, and William Booth were on the cutting edge of evangelism. In the twentieth century, the major, long-term leader of evangelism has been Billy Graham. Evangelist Graham is a contemporary example of providing evangelistic leadership on its highest level to the world. He is bigger than life itself and is one of the most admired men in America. The respect for him and his ministry crosses all denominational barriers. Even unsaved and unchurched world leaders admire Evangelist Graham for his impeccable integrity and value to the world community.

There is solemn warning for every evangelist on the field today. Evangelists, though humble before God, must be certain while climbing the ladder of evangelistic leadership in the church that their ladder is not leaning against the wrong wall. How tragic it would be for evangelists to spend their whole life climbing the ladder of successful evangelism only to find at the end of life's perplexing journey that their unique God-ordained evangelistic role in the church was on another wall (see, for example, Covey and Waitley). Evangelists must know why they are where they are (motive) and where they are going in the future (mission).

The Pentecostal evangelist is to be the pacesetter in the church. The goal is world evangelization. The lack of time, before the coming of Christ, demands that evangelists be efficient, get the job done right the first time. The value of a soul requires effectiveness, getting the right job done. The evangelist's loyalty to Christ instills excellence, getting the right job done right. Someone has said, "If we do not have time to do it right the first time, when will we have time do it over?" When short men cast long shadows, then the sun is about to set. The sun is setting on the harvest field. Are you a pacesetter in evangelism? If not, then who? If not now, then when?

The Practicalities of Evangelistic Leadership

The following chart (Figure 5) is a composite picture of a national evangelists' survey. There was a dual purpose for conducting such a survey: first, to reveal to pastors the uniqueness of the life and ministry of the evangelist; sec-

Survey of Active Evangelists

1. Length of ministry on the evangelistic field?
   a. Under one year (4.6%)
   b. 1–5 years (27.9%)
   c. 5–10 years (20.8%)
   d. More than 10 years (46.7%)

2. Times you speak per year?
   a. 0–100 (20.6%)
   b. 101–150 (17.5%)
   c. 151–200 (24.7%)
   d. 201–250 (18.6%)
   e. More than 250 (18.6%)

3. Do you have a full evangelistic schedule?
   a. Yes (72.7%)
   b. No (27.3%)

4. Years required to have a full preaching schedule?
   a. 0–3 years (80.1%)
   b. 4–6 years (14.4%)
   c. More than 6 years (5.5%)

5. Percentage of services from contacting pastors?
   a. 0–25% (37.4%)
   b. 26–50% (14.4%)
   c. 51–75% (15.4%)
   d. 76–100% (32.8%)

6. Percentage of services by invitations from pastors?
   a. 0–25% (46.4%)
   b. 26–50% (17.3%)
   c. 51–75% (11.7%)
   d. 76–100% (24.5%)

7. Years to achieve financial stability?
   a. 0–3 years (45.8%)
   b. 4–6 years (13.2%)
   c. More than 6 years (7.9%)
   d. Not making it (33.2%)

8. Do you have health insurance?
   a. Yes (65.8%)
   b. No (34.2%)

9. What is your gross income from evangelism?
   a. $10,000 or less (22.8%)
   b. $10,001–$24,999 (32.6%)
   c. $25,000–$39,999 (20.2%)
   d. $40,000–$59,999 (7.3%)
   e. $60,000–$79,999 (8.8%)
   f. $80,000 or more (8.3%)

10. Cancellations you receive per year?
    a. 0–5 (80.4%)
    b. 6–9 (16.0%)
    c. 10 or more (3.6%)

11. What is your main target audience?
    a. Children (8.6%)
    b. Youth (13.2%)
    c. Adult (87.0%)
    d. Other (11.2%)

12. What are the top needs of evangelists? (Top three)
    a. Finances (78.2%)
    b. Intimacy with God (66.0%)
    c. Respect (41.6%)

13. Effects of evangelistic life on family?
    a. Not difficult (35.4%)
    b. Somewhat difficult (28.1%)
    c. Average difficulty (24.7%)
    d. Difficult (6.7%)
    e. Very difficult (5.1%)

14. Percentage of return ministry?
    a. 0–33% (22.7%)
    b. 34–66% (40.2%)
    c. 67% or more (37.1%)

15. New sermons prepared per year?
    a. 1–5 (11.8%)
    b. 6–10 (28.2%)
    c. 11 or more (60.0%)

16. Kinds of sermons you preached most?
    a. Topical (38.8%)
    b. Expository (36.2%)
    c. Illustrative (15.3%)
    d. Other (9.7%)

17. Bible college or seminary graduate?
    a. Yes (56.9%)
    b. No (43.1%)

Percentages may not total 100% due to rounding and/or to multiple responses on the questionnaire.

Figure 5. Final response summary of evangelists' survey.

ond, to determine the average years required to move through the various phases of evangelistic leadership. The evangelist faces unique challenges pertaining to even having the opportunity to fulfill the biblical purpose and pattern for this ministry gift in the body of Christ.

The life and ministry of the evangelist is physically, domestically, financially, mentally, and spiritually demanding. The evangelist's lifestyle is physically difficult because of the annual preaching schedule. Out of all the active evangelists, 37.2 percent preach more than 200 times per year, or between 4 and 6 times per week. Only someone who has preached more than 200 times per year for a number of years can imagine the cumulative physical stress of effective nightly ministry.

It is hard to comprehend the spiritual battles of full-time evangelists. The number two need among evangelists is "intimacy with God." In some ways, evangelists, like most ministers, live overcrowded lives. The contemporary evangelist is bombarded with more responsibilities than the evangelist of a generation ago. The motel is not only a place to sleep but also a prayer chamber and a fully functioning office.

CROSS REFERENCES OF SURVEY

With these overall statistics in mind, question 1 on the survey (see page 109) was also cross-referenced with questions 2, 5, 6, 7, 9, and 14. This cross-referencing was done to further clarify the average time required to progress through the various stages of evangelistic leadership. Some evangelists progress faster than others through the various phases. In any case, I advocate the long view for developing an effective evangelistic preaching ministry.

There are two main criteria for determining whether an evangelist is ministering at the permission phase or the production phase in the church. The first criteria is the preaching schedule. What is considered a full-time preaching schedule? For an evangelist to be considered full-time and to be financially successful, I believe more than two hundred speaking opportunities per year are required. Research shows the longer the evangelist is on the field, the fuller the calendar will be. When question 1 of the survey is cross-referenced with questions 5 and 6, the average evangelist requires 6 or more years to develop a full schedule. A very small percent of the "1–5 years" are speaking more than 200 times per year, 39.1 percent of the "6–10 years" evangelists are speaking more than 200 times per year, and 52.2 percent of the "more than ten years" are speaking

The life and ministry of the evangelist is demanding.

more than 200 times per year. If evangelists are to move to higher levels of leadership in the church at large, then their ministries must be effective on a weekly basis in local churches.

Furthermore, for most evangelists to maintain a full schedule, they will have to continue making initial contacts with pastors and others about possible evangelism opportunities. However, with the process of progression and length of tenure on the field, the necessity of making initial contacts (50 percent or more of the time) will continue to decrease throughout time. For example, evangelists who have been traveling between "1–5 years" report that they make the initial contact with pastors 55.5 percent of the time to maintain at least half of their full-time schedule. Evangelists who have been traveling "10 years or more" contact pastors only 44.5 percent of the time to maintain full-time schedules.

The longer evangelists have been conducting effective local church crusades, the higher their "return ministry" among the churches. The "return ministry" of 67 percent or more for evangelists in the "1–5 years" category is 18.9 percent; for evangelists in the "6–10 years" category, 31.7 percent; and for evangelists in the "10 or more years" category, 50.5 percent. There is a saying: "If a pastor is not willing to have an evangelist back, why should the next pastor be willing to have the evangelist the first time?"

This survey should erase the myth of evangelists and large profits.

It is reasonable to conclude that when evangelists cross the bridge of the majority of opportunities resulting from invitations versus the making of initial contacts, then they have progressed from the permission phase to the production phase in the church at large. The evangelist is becoming better known for "results" on a broader scale.

Furthermore, the longer an evangelist sows, the more stable the financial base. There is a decrease in the number of evangelists "not making it" in each category of "1–5 years," "6–10 years," and "10 or more years."

As a result of this extensive survey, the myth of evangelists pocketing large sums of revenue should be erased from people's minds. The financial burden of evangelists fluctuates like the Dow Jones average. A summary of their financial portfolio is as follows: (1) 22.8 percent of itinerant ministers earn less than $10,000 per year, (2) 55.4 percent of all evangelists earn less than $25,000 per year, (3) 34.2 percent do not have health insurance, and (4) 33.2 percent are not making it financially on the evangelistic field (see Figure 5). This survey illuminates the financial hardships of evangelists today. Is it any wonder why evangelists indicated that their number one need is "finances"? If you are a pastor, please be generous with your visiting evangelist.

Within the first five years of evangelism, less than 10 percent of evangelists report making $39,999 or more per year. For those who have been itinerating between six and ten years, more than two-thirds (70.8 percent) are still making less than $40,000 a year. In ten or more years of evangelism, only a few of them (3.1 percent) have crossed the $39,999 barrier. Stable finances and a full schedule of services are the two greatest challenges facing evangelists today. Anyone seeking a career in evangelism for financial gain will be greatly disappointed. I asked earlier, if money was not an issue and time was plentiful, what would you spend the rest of your life doing for Christ? You must know your calling in life.

To establish the average years required to develop an effective evangelistic ministry, the "permission and production phases" must be clearly defined. When an evangelist receives an invitation for ministry from a pastor, this is a picture of the production phase in the church. When an evangelist must initiate the contact for ministry with the pastor, then it is a picture of the permission phase in the local churches. The number of speaking venues per year is a further indication of the demand for ministry by a particular evangelist.

Most evangelists do not receive enough invitations from pastors to maintain a full schedule. Only about a quarter (24.5 percent) of all evangelists are able to maintain a full-time evangelistic preaching ministry strictly from invitations alone. Almost half (48.2 percent) must initiate contacts in order to fill half of their crusade schedules. Thus, most evangelists are ministering on the permission level and not the production level.

According to the overall respondents' answers, 80.1 percent of the evangelists needed between 0 to 3 years, and 19.9 percent needed 4 or more years to move from the position phase through the permission phase to the production phase in the church (see Figure 5). But even though these statistics may represent a full schedule, they do not necessarily reflect the corresponding level of evangelistic leadership in the church. For the majority of evangelists, a full schedule is the result of a combination of initiation and invitation. These corresponding percentages were specified above. When one evaluates all the data, the average evangelist requires approximately five years to move from the position phase, through the permission phase, to the production phase.

As it relates to financial stability, 45.8 percent of the evangelists indicated that it took 0 to 3 years, and 21.2 percent stated that 4 or more years were required to reach fiscal consistency. Yet, as stated earlier, 33.2 percent of all evangelists are *not making it financially* on the field. However, these financial figures do not reflect the percentage of spouses working to underwrite their livelihood and evangelism efforts.

The people development phase and personhood phase are attained only after an evangelist has biblically built, skillfully executed, and creatively equipped the church for evangelism for decades. These last two phases are beyond the reach of this research.

Further, the statistics of this survey do not measure the level of intelligence, degree of determination, amount of creativity, willingness to sacrifice, or depth of the Christian life in order to develop cutting-edge evangelistic leadership in the church as a whole.

Such qualities are the private matters of evangelism. The statistics indicate only that the majority of evangelists are conducting their evangelistic ministries on level two (permission phase) and are finding it very difficult to move to a higher level of effective ministry. These are some of the public matters of evangelism indicating, as a whole, a less-than-desirable composite picture of evangelists.

Evangelism Exercises

1. What are the differences between a manager and a leader?
2. What is evangelistic leadership?
3. What are the five levels of evangelistic leadership? Describe each level.
4. Where are you on the five levels of evangelistic leadership? How can you move to the next level?
5. What are the differences between "springboards" and "sounding boards"? List five people in each category.
6. Where are you leading in evangelism and where are you being led in evangelism by others?
7. How can the statistics from the evangelists survey help you with your evangelistic ministry?

8

The Priorities of the Evangelist

It has been said, "We do not see things as they are but as we are." Every person views life through a personal lens or paradigm. "Derived from the Greek word *paradeigma,* meaning 'model,' a paradigm is a way of understanding the world. It is a pattern or set of guidelines that influences the way you look at your life" (Waitley, 1). Since individuals have their own paradigm and no one can fully understand or see through the lens of another individual, life is lived with question marks. For example, unless someone has traveled for an extended period, it is virtually impossible to understand the lifestyle of an itinerant minister.

The Defining of Priorities

Once evangelists have decided their God-given purpose based upon the principles of the New Testament evangelist, they are ready to develop their priorities for effective evangelism. Priorities come before prioritization. Priorities paint the full picture of an individual's purpose. Even though principles remain constant and purpose will be fine-tuned throughout the years, priorities change as one's evangelistic ministry expands. Priorities are the bridge between an evangelist's or a pastor's purpose and programs for evangelism. Priorities are a reflection of one's values in life and ministry. Priorities represent the overall building of an effective evangelistic preaching ministry.

The Development of Priorities

How does one develop and manage the priorities for his or her personal life and professional evangelistic or pastoral ministry? Instead of focusing on acquiring things and saving time, strive to preserve and deepen relationships and accomplish results. The Pareto Principle, commonly called the 80/20 principle (based on Italian economist/sociologist Vilfredo Pareto's discovery that some 80 percent of desired results will flow from approximately 20 percent of one's activities), and time management are two efficient and effective ways to prioritize the evangelist's life and ministry.

The Pareto Principle states: "Twenty percent of your priorities will give you 80 percent of your production, if you spend your time, energy, money, and personnel on the top 20 percent of your priorities" (Maxwell, 20). This principle can also be applied to the family, recreation, and other pursuits in life. If you are just beginning an evangelistic ministry, you may not fully understand the potential impact (negative or positive) of this formula on your evangelistic ministry. The formula based upon the 80/20 principle for prioritizing your professional evangelistic ministry priorities is as follows:

1. Discover the top 20 percent of the evangelists and pas-

tors in your life. Research and write them down.

2. Decide to spend 80 percent of your "people time" with the top 20 percent of evangelists and pastors in your life. Develop relationships with them.

3. Develop avenues for spending 80 percent of your personal development money on the top 20 percent of the evangelists and pastors. Invest in other ministries.

4. Determine what 20 percent of the work gives 80 percent of the return and train an assistant (a friend, family member, or a member of your local church) to do the 80 percent less-effective work. This allows you to do what you do best in your evangelistic ministry.

5. Delegate to the top 20 percent of evangelists and pastors to do on-the-job training for the next 20 percent of evangelists and pastors. This level of prioritizing will be not be available to you until after many years of developing deep respect and trust in the church at large (Maxwell, 22).

How can you discover who the top 20 percent of the high achievers are who have a direct or indirect impact on your evangelistic ministry in the Pentecostal church? Make a list of everyone who has some form of association with your evangelism efforts (evangelists, pastors, and key lay leaders). Then carefully read down the list, placing a check mark by those whose support will help, or whose nonsupport will hurt, your evangelism efforts. If their support or nonsupport of you will not affect your evangelism efforts, then do not place a check mark by their names. Upon completion of this simple exercise, you will know the top 20 percent of the high achievers who can help you accomplish your evangelistic purpose and priorities in the Pentecostal church.

Time management is another tool to build an effective evangelistic preaching ministry. Evangelists and pastors must never treat things like people and people like things. Efficiency comes through things but effectiveness comes through people. In his book *The Seven Habits of Highly Effective People,* Stephen R. Covey maintains that time can be diagrammed into four quadrants as illustrated by the following Matrix:

Figure 6. Time Management Matrix®.

	URGENT	NOT URGENT
IMPORTANT	**I** **Activities** • Crises • Pressing problems • Deadline-driven projects, meetings, preparations	**II** **Activities** • Preparation • Prevention • Values clarification • Planning • Relationship building • Recreation • Empowerment
NOT IMPORTANT	**III** **Activities** • Interruptions, some phone calls • Some mail, some reports • Many proximate, pressing matters • Many popular activities	**IV** **Activities** • Trivia, busywork • Junk mail • Time wasters • Escape activities

Time Management Matrix is a registered trademark of Franklin Covey Co. Trademark and copyrighted material used with permission.

Often ministers are committed to doing urgent things faster not realizing they are moving slower toward accomplishing the important things in life. There is a vast difference between prioritizing according to the urgent things and prioritizing according to the most important things! Often urgent things involve immediate responsibilities and important things involve intimate relationships.

The simple truth regarding time management is that life is made of four quadrants. Covey maintains that Quadrant II consists of the most important activities in life. When a person neglects Quadrant II activities, those activities will eventually become crises (Quadrant I). Most individuals' time is wasted in Quadrants III and IV.

As soon as finances allow, an assistant, secretary, or voluntary local church person should be assigned these duties to free the evangelist to focus on Quadrant II for effective evangelism. The evangelist and the pastor must not settle for "good things" in life instead of the "best things." If they are not careful, the good things will become bad things because they will rob the itinerant minister of the best things God has prepared for their ministry. Ministers have the sacred responsibility of leveraging their time for personal and public effectiveness. "It is easy to say 'no!' when there's a deeper 'yes!' burning inside" (Covey, 103).

The Description of Some Priorities

The following priorities are intended to crystallize for evangelists and pastors the behind-the-scenes life of the evangelist. This is not intended to be an exhaustive list. Your priorities will no doubt include the following list, but you will also have unique priorities that fit only your roles and goals and mission and vision.

"If only I had more time" sums up the difference between failure and success. Yet the truth is that God never intended for us to do everything. Many evangelists live overcrowded lives, without a "margin" for error or failure. Richard Swenson describes the concept of margin this way:

> The conditions of modern-day living devour margin. If you are homeless, we direct you to a shelter. If you are penniless, we offer you food stamps. If you are breathless, we connect the oxygen. But if you are marginless, we give you yet one more thing to do.
>
> Marginless is being thirty minutes late to the doctor's office because you were twenty minutes late getting out of the hairdresser's because you were ten minutes late dropping the children off at school because the car ran out of gas two blocks from the gas station—and you forgot your purse.
>
> Margin, on the other hand, is having breath left at the top of the staircase, money left at the end of the month, and sanity left at the end of adolescence.
>
> Marginless is the baby crying and the phone ringing at the same time; margin is Grandma taking the baby for the afternoon.
>
> Marginless is being asked to carry a load five pounds heavier than you can lift; margin is a friend to carry half the burden.
>
> Marginless is not having time to finish the book you're reading on stress; margin is having the time to read it twice.
>
> Marginless is fatigue; margin is energy.
>
> Marginless is red ink; margin is black ink.
>
> Marginless is anxiety; margin is security.
>
> Marginless is culture; margin is counterculture.
>
> Marginless is reality; margin is remedy.
>
> Marginless is the disease of the 1990s.
>
> Margin is its cure (Swenson, 13–14).

Are you living a marginless ministry? If twenty-first-century evangelists are going to tackle all of the nagging demands of the busy life of evangelism, they must practice the right priorities.

The first priority of the evangelist is *faith in God.* Billy Graham has said, "Evangelists are activists. Traveling, meeting new people, organizing, and preaching keeps us busy. But we need to remember that it is not so much our activity for Christ as our captivity to Him which is most important" (Graham, 81). As the influence of an evangelist deepens in the church, greater physical and spiritual demands are made upon him or her. Private time with God must constantly be guarded. An evangelist needs godly wisdom and spiritual discipline to maintain the balance of study, prayer, personal growth, health, and administration while traveling full-time today. Normal community life does not exist for the full-time, itinerant preacher.

The evangelist needs to be accountable to the pastor during the week of crusade services. Evangelists should insulate themselves from the world but not isolate themselves from their fellow laborers in the harvest field. There needs to be a well-balanced association between the evangelist and the pastor. It is most appropriate for the pastor to help you guard your spiritual life during the church crusade. The pastor should permit the evangelist flexibility during the week to study and pray for the nightly services and to provide time for a devotional life with Christ.

The second priority of the evangelist is *family.* If the itinerant minister travels alone, the family is without a parent/spouse most of the year. They too have sacrificed along with the evangelist to seek and save the lost. A burden for those without Christ, invitations to preach the gospel, and the financial concerns of the ministry often make it difficult for the itinerant preacher to remain home for extended periods of time (Graham, 99).

If the evangelist's family travels as well, the husband and wife must guard the sanctity of their home. The family needs a sense of normalcy while on the field. Since the evangelist needs to study and pray for upcoming services, then a place of study should be sought at the church office to give the family time to breathe during the day. If the hotel room is the living quarters for the evangelist and family, then it should not become the constant office for life on the road. The home life should be protected at all costs. Of course, exceptions and crises do arise. Yet, do not let "marginless" overcome "margin."

Before leaving home, the evangelist should consider planning special events for the family while they are on the road. Cultivate a sense of expectancy. Itinerant ministry can be exciting for the family. Occasionally, give your family a night off from the crusade. Plan for the long road ahead and not just the next turn on the calendar. Think of creative ways to turn the hotel room into a home. It can be done, but it requires discipline and godly decision making.

The home life should be protected at all cost.

The third priority of the evangelist is *fitness*. The evangelist lives in changing locations with different surroundings, unfamiliar sleeping conditions, a new schedule with a new pastor, and new food nearly every week. It is difficult to maintain a routine of exercise, much less other normal patterns of life. An individual has to be flexible in order to meet the unique demands of this ministry. One of the mottoes of the effective evangelist is: "Blessed are the flexible, for they will not be easily bent out of shape." This is a crucial concern for the evangelist and for the longevity of ministry. The evangelist needs to plan for times of recreation during weekly evangelistic crusades. If not, the physical crises of quadrant one will overwhelm the possibility of long-term evangelism.

Besides being physically fit, the evangelist must be professionally fit, understanding that the motel has become both the home and office most of the year. The twenty-first-century evangelist will maintain a fully functional office while on the road, in the air, or in the hotel. No doubt, correspondence will be maintained with a portable notebook computer and printer. Cost-effective cell phone networks and electronic mail will make the evangelist accessible anywhere in the world. Faxes can be sent and received in the privacy of the hotel room without even going to the registration desk. Computer desktop publishing will make it possible to design and print newsletters out of town, and financial programs with on-line banking will permit up-to-the-minute bookkeeping while away from home. The Bible and sermon software of the twenty-first century will make it possible to engage in sermon preparation with full access to theological libraries throughout the world via the Internet. Just as the local church has an ongoing office during the crusade, the motel room will become a fully functional office for the evangelist. The pastor and the evangelist together must decide how to put first things first individually and corporately during the evangelistic crusade for maximum results.

The fourth priority of the evangelist is *finance.* Even though evangelists typically may not speak freely about finances, they are greatly concerned about them. If the pastor does not approach the evangelist about the finances of the crusade, then the evangelist needs to ask graciously if love offerings will be received during the services.

Evangelists will need to maintain a home residence with the expenses of a mortgage, lawn care, taxes, utilities, and a ministry office, even though they are often gone. Furthermore, evangelists need to maintain an automobile. If itinerants travel long distances by automobile, they will need a large, roadworthy vehicle. If they fly, they will probably need the church to cover this expense in advance. If there are two or three days free time between meetings, then motel and food costs will be an additional financial burden.

Moreover, evangelists have medical, auto, and house insurance premiums. They are forced to endure many weeks without income due to certain holidays when churches have their own special activities. Many churches do not schedule evangelists from Thanksgiving to New Year's, on holiday weekends, or in the summertime.

Evangelists do not receive a Christmas bonus from the church, paid expenses to ministerial functions, vacation and sick pay, or reimbursement for office expenses. These are some of the financial realities of the evangelist's life and ministry. Thus, evangelists must be careful to budget their money and not overextend themselves.

The fifth priority of the evangelist is the *future*. If you do not know where you are going in life, then it does not matter if the alarm clock sounds on time for you. What gets you up each morning? What are your priorities in ministry?

How can you do it? First, evaluate your priorities each month. Are the requirements worth the reward? Second, eliminate those priorities someone else could do for you. Third, estimate how long your top projects of the month will take then plan your time accordingly (Maxwell, 28).

Evangelism Exercises

1. What does the term *paradigm* mean?
2. What are two ways to develop and manage your priorities? Memorize them.
3. What are the differences between "margin" and "marginless"? Write down areas where you are outside the margin in the ministry or family life.
4. What are five major priorities of evangelists?
5. Why do you set your alarm clock in the morning? What is your life-forming goal?
6. How can you continue to update your priorities?

9

The Pastor and the Evangelist

As an evangelist, I have been afforded the opportunity of traveling more than two million miles to date in ministry worldwide. I have been privileged to preach the gospel in more than five hundred churches in America. Over the years, I have made it a practice to listen to and learn from, to watch and write about, cutting-edge pastors and churches. One overarching principle I have observed through these hundreds of crusades is this: *The more we synergize, the more we can evangelize.* This principle is true on the local, district, national, and international levels.

Unity can be achieved in one of two different ways in the local church. An organization is either melded together or frozen together. The first produces vitality and the second mortality. The first focuses on the future and the second focuses on the past. The philosophy of twenty-first-century evangelism should be *Everybody is a somebody in the body of Christ.*

The pastor and the evangelist can accomplish more together than they can by themselves. They can add value to each other's ministry and in turn add more value together to the local church. The evangelist needs to realize the importance of the office of the pastor before and during a local church crusade. Just as the husband-wife relationship must be nurtured in order to grow harmoniously, the pastor-evangelist relationship must be cultivated to develop mutual trust. However, this pastor-evangelist relationship continuum is even more difficult to achieve due to the distance between the two having these ministry gifts. The synergistic mind-set must diminish all distances and time restraints for effective evangelism to occur in the local church. So how do evangelists and pastors develop long-lasting relationships for the purpose of equipping the saints and evangelizing the lost?

Trust

Trust and trustworthiness are foundational to building evangelist-pastor relationships. These character qualities are developed in the private life before the public life. The evangelist cannot establish credibility in the church if trust is violated in the eyes of the local pastor. In order to reverse the declining credibility of the evangelist in the church, itinerant ministers must guard their sacred trust given by Christ. When one ministry gift found in Ephesians 4:11 suffers, all ministry gifts ultimately suffer in their "work of service." Without a doubt the credibility of the evangelist is at an all-time low in America. "The tarnish on the image of the evangelist desperately needs removal and the luster restored" (Drummond, 68).

Evangelists must continue to cultivate their character.

Image and integrity, however, are not of equal value. Image is found in the arena of public opinion, but integrity is found in the heart of a person. Image is how people know the evangelist, but integrity is how God knows the evangelist.

There is one simple way to establish trust on the local, district, national, and international levels of evangelism: *consistency*. Consistency builds credibility. Credibility builds confidence in the minds of people.

Transparency

Ask pastors how you can become more relevant, resourceful, and reliable in your crusade evangelism. Be transparent with them if you expect them to be transparent with you. The deeper the pastor-evangelist relationship, the wider its effectiveness in evangelism.

Figure 7 (see page 132) lists statistical results of the national pastors' survey.

Pastors are searching for evangelists of integrity who have a solid Bible-preaching ministry with dynamic altar services. They consider a crusade successful when it contains Bible-based preaching followed by people being saved and baptized in the Holy Spirit. The two greatest challenges pastors face regarding evangelists are finding the right evangelist for their church and getting people to attend the crusade. Pastors believe there are two main ways evangelists can improve their effectiveness in the local church: relevant messages and dynamic altar services. The two biggest complaints pastors have about evangelists are that they are financially demanding and manipulative during the altar services. Pastors are also in a quandary about whom they should invite to their churches.

Evangelists should practice servanthood in all aspects of their ministry if they plan to advance the kingdom of God in the local church. The following admonition is applicable to all:

> A new moral principle is emerging which holds that the only authority deserving one's allegiance is that which is freely and knowingly granted by the led to the leader in response to, and in proportion to, the clearly evident servant stature of the leader. Those who choose to follow this principle will not casually accept the authority of existing institutions. Rather, they will freely respond only to individuals who are chosen as leaders because they are proven and trusted as servants (Greenleaf, 9–10).

A COMPARISON OF PASTORS' AND EVANGELISTS' SURVEYS

When the pastors' survey about evangelists and the evangelists' survey about their evangelism are compared, several striking conclusions emerge. First, the major criticism pastors have regarding evangelists is that they are financially demanding. There is a great paradox in evangelism. If an evangelist requires a certain honorarium for ministry too soon, then rejection is sure to come from pastors. However, if that same evangelist will pay the price of faithful and fruitful ministry, the day will come when a certain honorarium can be required and accepted by many pastors but will not be needed because the amount of the honorariums will be more than adequate to underwrite the evangelist's ministry. The higher the respect in the church, the higher the revenue from ministry. Earn respect in the church.

Second, pastors said the number one way evangelists can

Survey of Leading Pastors about Evangelists

1. Main qualities looked for in evangelists:
   a. Integrity (80.6%)
   b. Solid Bible preacher (70.1%)
   c. Fruitful ministry (60.2%)

2. Hosted a campaign within last year?
   a. Yes (80.6%)
   b. No (19.4%)

3. Was your last campaign successful?
   a. Yes (85.2%)
   b. No (14.8%)

4. Why was your campaign successful?
   a. Souls saved (60.7%)
   b. Holy Spirit baptisms (48.5%)
   c. Dynamic preaching (47.7%)

5. How often do you invite evangelists?
   a. 1–3 times per year (87.9%)
   b. 4+ times per year (6.3%)
   c. Never (5.8%)

6. Greatest challenge about evangelists:
   a. Right evangelist (54.7%)
   b. Attendance (37.0%)
   c. Finances (8.3%)

7. Negative characteristics of evangelists:
   a. Financially demanding (40.3%)
   b. Altar manipulation (36.3%)
   c. Nonservant (33.1%)

8. How can evangelists be more effective?
   a. Relevant message (74.6%)
   b. Dynamic altar services (72.9%)
   c. Better correspondence (21.8%)

9. Most desired evangelistic ministry:
   a. Holy Spirit emphasis (67.3%)
   b. Adult ministry (63.7%)
   c. Youth ministry (56.0%)

Percentages may not total 100% due to rounding and/or to multiple responses.

Figure 7. Final valid responses of pastors' survey.

improve their effectiveness would be to have a "relevant message" for the local church. Evangelists must stay contemporary with the rapidly changing times. In chapter 13, the evangelist and pastor learn the principles and practicalities of developing dynamic, life-changing messages that expound God's Word and exalt His Son.

Time

Evangelists and pastors can pick their choices but not their consequences. The consequences are in the hands of God. This is the law of the harvest. Birthing, building, and broadening a full-time evangelistic preaching ministry is not like an all-night cram session before a final exam.

Can you imagine a farmer procrastinating through the spring and summer, then cramming seed into the ground in the early fall, expecting a harvest before winter? Can you imagine an evangelist wasting time week after week, expecting an evangelistic ministry with bountiful fruit? Can you imagine a preacher never studying, never praying, never stretching the mind, never building relationships, never visiting the lost, and never developing leadership skills but still expecting to have a glowing, growing, and going evangelistic ministry? Can you imagine the pastor and evangelist working together in the harvest field but never communicating with each other? Evangelists and pastors cannot "excuse" themselves from something they acted themselves into during their life and ministry. Problems arise when evangelists sow one kind of commitment and expect something entirely different in the ministry. Evangelists must continually sow the seed of healthy, vibrant pastoral relationships if they plan to be successful on the evangelistic field.

Patience follows planting. Once the farmer has planted the seed, it must be given time to germinate. The farmer cannot uncover the seed to check on its root system. The farmer must water, cultivate, and protect the sown seed in order to receive a future harvest. Waiting time is not wasted time.

Evangelists need to be patient during their tenure on the evangelistic field. Much waiting and working are required on an annual basis. Cultivating close pastor-evangelist relationships and conducting consistent, successful local church crusades make up the bedrock for building an evangelistic ministry. Shortcuts do not pay off in the long run. If one practices the principles of the farm, then harvest will come one day. When that day of harvest opportunity arrives, the evangelist must be ready to seize it for bountiful results.

Evangelism Exercises

1. What is the philosophy of twenty-first-century evangelism?
2. How can an evangelist develop a meaningful relationship with a pastor?
3. What are the differences between image and integrity?
4. According to pastors, what are the two ways evangelists can improve their effectiveness in evangelism?
5. How can an evangelist be compared to a farmer? What are some areas in your ministry that need cultivating for future fruitfulness?

10

The Practics of the Evangelist

How many times has a father tried to put together his child's toy without reading the instructions? How many times have people tried to operate a new computer program without studying the handbook? Just like most children's toys have nuts and bolts and most computer programs have diskettes and CD-ROMs, the evangelistic ministry has specific paradigms and practices for successful evangelism. There are four main areas.

Marketing

In secular terms, you own and operate a small business in America. Even though you may call it a "ministry," America calls it a business. If you are just beginning your evangelistic ministry, you are establishing "YOU, Inc." (see Figure 8, page 144). Everything you do, say, or buy will either add to or subtract from your ministry. If you will invest wisely in YOU, Inc., there will be dividends of ministry for years to come.

How do evangelists become known throughout an entire denomination? How can they expand ministry boundaries without being pushy with pastors? First, they must determine their uniqueness in the church. Each evangelist must be able to answer the questions: "Why should pastors have me in their local churches?" "What do I have to offer that no other evangelist has to offer today?" "What is that 'one

Do not advertise something you cannot deliver. That is false advertisement!

thing' I have to give that sets me apart from other itinerant ministries?" "What do I want to be known for in the church?" If an evangelist does not clearly answer these questions, then his or her advertisement will not clearly reflect the differences from other ministries. Advertisement should be built on answers to the above and other similar questions.

Second, evangelists need to be creative in their advertisement. Advertisement consists of newsletters, press releases, ad slicks for newspapers and church bulletins, videos, pictures, brochures, posters, business cards, and other products for use by the pastor and the local church. Promotional materials should reflect the answers to the following questions: (1) Why are we having the upcoming crusade? (2) Who are we trying to reach in this crusade? (3) What is this crusade about? (4) When will this crusade begin? (5) Where will this crusade be held?

Even though respect and integrity are separate and are more important than reputation and image, reputation and image make up the marketing side of ministry. A person must earn respect, yet that person's reputation is often a matter of perception. An evangelist must earn respect, yet in the church at large, reputation is understood by perception. Integrity is an issue of the heart before God, but image must be "packaged" for the church. You want the perception to be made up of the mission of your ministry, while the package is made up of the methods for advertising that ministry. Your goal is to bring together both the churches' perception and your packaging. The packaging of the "product" (effective ministry) will produce either a positive or negative perception of the evangelist by the pastor. Do not advertise something you cannot deliver. That is false advertisement!

Third, creatively develop a name and logo for YOU, Inc. They should represent your entire emphasis in the church at large. Do not name the ministry after yourself. If you are not convinced of the power of symbols, analyze them on the merchandise you purchase. Consider having a professional artist design your ministry logo. There is a vast difference between having an idea and knowing how to market that idea. You may have an idea and make only one dollar, or you may have an idea and make a million dollars. That is the difference between ideas and marketing. There are millions of ideas but not many million-dollar ideas.

Fourth, evangelists need a plan to make it known that YOU, Inc. is "open for business." Develop creative ways to present your ministry to pastors. Filter your advertising plan through the five levels of evangelistic leadership (see chapter 7). Design a Web page on the Internet. Gather recommendations from key spiritual influencers in the church.

Target specific perceived needs in the local church. Mail your materials to pastors. Give your materials to pastor-friends and ask them to mail them to their friends. Advertise in Christian magazines. Evaluate both secular and sacred advertisements to learn the principles of others' success.

When beginning an evangelistic ministry, take the initiative to contact pastors instead of expecting them to contact you. It is more advantageous to write a pastor first with materials about your ministry that have been printed professionally. If you phone a pastor and he or she is not in the office, ascertain another time to call. Pastors get lots of calls, so be patient. Upon the completion of each evangelistic crusade, regardless of the amount of the offering, always write a thank-you to the pastor.

Materials

There are three kinds of printed materials: the kind that is immediately thrown away upon arrival, the kind that is good enough to stay out of the trash but not good enough to be shown to guests, and the kind that qualifies for the coffee table. What kind of printed materials do you want representing YOU, Inc.?

Imagine your newsletter being in the morning mail of pastors. What first catches the attention of the pastor or church secretary? What will make them want to read it? Will they place it in the file marked "future guests," or, better yet, will they create a file labeled YOU, Inc.? Think long and hard about these questions. Develop a long-term marketing strategy for your materials.

Revise your printed materials at least every two years.

Use updated photographs. Do not allow your materials to appear cheap. Excellence without extravagance is the goal in ministry-oriented materials. With the lowering prices of computers and laser printers, it is now possible to have the latest technology for producing high-quality materials at reasonable prices. In the twenty-first century, there will be low tolerance for halfhearted, slipshod printed materials in the church. Strive to produce your newsletters, video and tape series covers, and posters in full color. Always remember that everything you mail has your fingerprints on it and your personality in it.

Money

On the one hand, some evangelists blame their problems on the church at large and the pastor in particular. They say their lack of financial resources is the fault of others who are not fulfilling their responsibilities to evangelists. Even though some churches have taken advantage of or neglected evangelists, itinerant ministers must ultimately create such a persona that respect will replace rejection and notice will replace neglect. Is this possible? Yes!

On the other hand, some evangelists have more financial resources available to them than do other evangelists, yet their finances still do not underwrite their evangelistic dreams. Their ministry is on one level, but their dreams are on a higher level. They are always climbing higher mountains and seeing bigger and brighter horizons. Why do you want more finances? Is it for security or for service?

If you are beginning an evangelistic preaching ministry, establish biblical principles of stewardship. Study the Bible on money and materialism. Attend financial improvement seminars. Contact a local Christian accountant or attorney and determine the most advantageous way to register your ministry organization as a nonprofit entity on both the state and federal levels. These measures will further ensure accountability and increased revenues from those who desire to contribute to your ministry. The extra time and money spent here is a wise investment for your future ministry.

Set up a business checking account separate from your personal account. Pay yourself a salary and all business expenses from your ministry account. Keep accurate records and business receipts. During the early years, there may be weeks when you cannot even pay yourself. Do not be discouraged. Request the local church to write your honorarium check out to your ministry name and not to you personally. This will save you countless tax dollars. You will be subject to taxes only when you draw a salary from your ministry account. Read books and magazines to stay current with tax law changes. You, not your accountant, are responsible for your finances.

Use an effective business computer program for your finances. Shop around and ask a lot of questions. Consult your accountant. A computer program will simplify financial computations, balance monthly bank statements, enhance exactness, save time, print checks, organize tax records, and make available online banking.

If you make a million dollars and spend a million dollars, you are still broke in a business sense. After you pay your tithes, you must pay your future first and save money now.

Be a wise investor of your finances. Get the facts. Diversify. Start early so compounding interest can work harder for you now. Then you will not have to work harder later in life. You can either pay now and play later or play now and pay later, but everyone must pay in life. The ideal way is to develop a financial strategy that will eventually provide you the opportunity to evangelize because you want to and not because you have to.

Do not overextend yourself on the evangelistic field. Monitor your average weekly offerings for a year before purchasing additional assets (house, car, land, etc.). Each year compare the previous year's earnings with your present earnings. Create a graph of your yearly finances. This will constantly provide an accurate picture of your financial stability.

The more financial tributaries flowing into your river of revenue, the more successful you will be monetarily on the field. Provide resource materials (tapes, books, videos) for people to purchase during the crusade services. Write a contemporary book or write for contemporary periodicals. Preach different sermon series and package them for Christians and non-Christians. However, always remember you are first a servant of God and not a salesperson of the church. Be tasteful and tactful when mentioning your resource materials from the platform. Consider the effect on unsaved people hearing the promotion of the products. Are they turned off before ever hearing you preach the gospel? If Christians or non-Christians do not first believe in the evangelist, they most likely will not purchase his or her resource materials. Higher respect equals higher revenue.

Above all else, never rob God by not paying tithes or giving generous offerings. Set the example in your giving during the local church crusade. When the offering plate or bag is passed, demonstrate your giving. If you are not willing to invest your money in your ministry, do not expect other people to invest their money in your ministry either.

Morale

All evangelists have challenging days financially. There are going to be periods when cancellations outnumber invitations. You will know the thrill of victory and the agony of defeat. You are not alone. Learn to fail forward instead of backward. Grow both spiritually and mentally through the lean times. Determine to turn your hard times into high times.

What activates you (your purpose) in evangelism will determine what motivates you (your passion) in evangelism. Your emotional equilibrium will be balanced when your purpose and passion work together. Emotional burnout results from the long-term imbalance of juggling purpose and passion without fulfilling any of your life-forming dreams and goals.

Place a high value on your God-given, evangelistic ministry. If you do not value your ministry, others will take advantage of it. Think more positive thoughts than negative thoughts. You are heading in the direction of your most dominating thoughts today, tomorrow, and in the future.

Evangelists must exercise faith for their finances. We must remember that Jesus did not have a place to lay His head. The Seventy were to depend upon the Lord of the harvest for their sleeping accommodations, food, and finances.

Philip conducted citywide crusades without any scriptural indication of financial support. The apostle Paul said:

> I know how to get along with humble means, and I also know how to live in prosperity; in any and every circumstance I have learned the secret of being filled and going hungry, both of having abundance and suffering need. I can do all things through Him who strengthens me (Phil. 4:12–13).

In the final analysis, let the following words of an anonymous poet ring loudly in your heart throughout your years in evangelism:

I counted dollars while God counted crosses.
I counted gains while He counted losses.
I counted my worth by the things gained and stored;
He sized me up by the scars that I wore.
I coveted honors and degrees;
He wept as He counted the hours I spent on my knees.
I never knew until one day by the grave
How vain are the things we spend our lives to save.

Evangelism Exercises

1. Do you have a marketing strategy?
2. Have you tried anything new in the last year?
3. Would you purchase your own resource materials if you were a layperson? Why or why not?
4. How many tributaries are flowing into your river of revenue? Name them. What new tributaries would you like to add in the next year? How can you make that happen?
5. Are you paying your future first?
6. Are you discouraged? What are some ways to keep your morale up? Are you practicing them?

YOU, INC.

MARKETING	MATERIALS	MONEY	MORALE
Purpose Why are you marketing your ministry?	**Target** Who do you want to impress and influence?	**Strategy** Are you paying your future first? What is your plan to add tributaries to your river of revenue?	**Spiritually** Do you love the Lord as much as the day you first gave your heart to Him?
Plan What is your strategy to become known in the church? Do you have any million-dollar ideas? How will you market them?	**Theme** What is the message of your ministry? Can you write it in one sentence? Is it memorable?	**Stewardship** Are you abiding by biblical principles? Are you charting your annual income?	**Emotionally** Are you emotionally balanced between what motivates you and what activates you in evangelism?
Packaging What is the logo? What is the image?	**Timely** Are you current with the culture?	**Saving** What percentage are saving? Where are you saving for your future?	**Mentally** Are you expanding your mind? Who challenges you?
Products What unique element do you have to offer the church?	**Trustworthy** Are your materials sensational or substantial?	**Successful** Are your annual earnings increasing each year?	**Physically** Do you have renewed energy? Are you healthy? What can you do to improve your health?

Figure 8. The practices of evangelism.

11

The Preparations for Evangelism

In today's world, more is required than a poster, a prayer, a pulpit, a program, a preacher, and a place to meet to attract both the saved and the unsaved to a local church crusade. As stated in chapter 2, the life and ministry of the evangelist not only includes the evangelization of the lost, but it also should incorporate the equipping of the saints to do the work of the ministry. It is advisable for the evangelist and the pastor to consider up-to-date techniques and leadership styles designed to win lost people to Christ. In many cases the evangelist will have to provide information and instructions to enable local churches to prepare properly for a crusade. The following preparations are intended to assist the evangelist, the pastor, and the local church in their evangelistic crusades and revival services.

Plan to Be Productive

It has often been said, "If we fail to plan, we are planning to fail." It is appropriate to expect more effort and energy to go into the creative phase than into the crusade phase.

Preparation comes before proclamation. Every goal requires a plan. The primary reason for planning is to coordinate the work of many people in order to ensure a successful crusade.

We are told that only 10 percent of an iceberg appears above the waterline while 90 percent is below. So the larger the 10 percent we see, the larger the 90 percent we don't see. Similarly, the more foundational work done before the crusade, the greater will be crusade results.

Do not allow tradition to be the main force behind an upcoming crusade. Just because the local church has always had a "spring crusade" does not mean that a young couple with school-age children will attend every night of the crusade. If possible, the evangelist and the pastor should schedule around conflicting events in the community. Avoiding unnecessary competition increases the likelihood of a successful evangelistic event.

Prioritize with Purpose

What is the purpose of the future crusade? Is it evangelism? Is it revival? The purpose of the crusade determines our priorities and our priorities determine our procedures. The following three questions will help both the evangelist and pastor focus on their purpose for an upcoming crusade:
1. Aim—Why are we having these crusade services?
2. Audience—Who are we trying to reach during this crusade?
3. Advertising—How are we going to make this crusade known to both the churched and the unchurched?

A farmer spends 80 to 90 percent of his time preparing

for the harvest. Only 10 percent of his time is actually spent in harvesting. The simple point is that quality sowing time will reap results in the local church. To change the analogy, no matter how skilled the obstetrician, if there has not been conception and gestation, the physician cannot deliver physical life. In the same manner, no matter how skilled the spiritual obstetrician, if there has not been a period of spiritual conception (purpose) and gestation (planning and promotion), new spiritual life will not be produced during the crusade. The pastor and evangelist should answer these two questions: What procedures need to be practiced in order to attract lost people to the crusade, and what will activate the whole congregation to be involved in it?

Promote for Participation

The pastor and the evangelist must do more than merely inform the congregation of an upcoming evangelistic event. They must instruct them about their participation in it. The pastor should consult the evangelist about what has worked in other churches to attract the unconverted to the crusade and to increase the involvement of the saints.

Every believer can be involved in some way to prepare for the gift of the evangelist to be exercised in the local church. Dr. Sterling Huston, Director of the North American Crusades for the Billy Graham Association, writes:

> Management experts tell us that involvement plus participation equals commitment. . . . Involvement in the process, and participation in the decisions, yields commitment toward the goals of any project. . . . The larger the number of people in some meaningful role in the preparations, the larger the number of people who will be influenced by these involved people. Each Christian

has a web of relationships about his life involving family, friends, neighbors, and acquaintances where he works, shops, or goes to school (Douglas, 237).

Thus, it is extremely important that specific plans be made to organize for recruitment within the local church to assure maximum involvement in the evangelistic event. Effective evangelism is the result of organizing people and executing procedures based on the priorities of the Bible.

There are several foundational approaches to promote participation in an effective evangelistic event. Dr. Huston has designed a fourfold crusade grid for citywide crusades (Douglas, 238–39). I have applied them to the local church evangelism effort. First, the pastor needs to *discover* who the key spiritual influencers are in the church. Think beyond titles or staff positions and ask who the main positive spiritual influencers are in the church. True effectiveness flows through people. The pastor should arrange an opportunity to discuss with these spiritual leaders the importance of evangelism and the upcoming crusade.

Second, after these key spiritual leaders have become committed to the crusade, the pastor or a key staff member needs to *delegate* responsibilities for the planned outreach. The pastor and this crusade committee should seek to involve as many people as possible in meaningful roles. Capable people must be selected who will commit themselves to a specific task equal to their talents. Each task must be clearly defined. There should be responsible individuals over music, counselors, finances, advertising, children's ministry, nursery, ushers, prayer, discipleship, prospective converts, etc.

Third, all persons recruited for involvement in an evangelistic event should be *developed* for their specific task. It is unfair to assume people know how to do what they have never been trained to do. As they are trained, they will gain a greater confidence in themselves and a deeper commitment to the crusade.

Fourth, whenever specific tasks are assigned, it is essential to specify *deadlines* for their completion. Deadlines force local church leaders to evaluate the progress of their preparations for the event. Included in these deadlines should be goals for every aspect of the crusade. These goals should be both realistic and faith-oriented. They should be large enough to stretch their faith in God and small enough for the congregation to buy into the planned crusade. Major goals should be set regarding prayer partners, advertising, attendance, finances, counselors, special music, etc. The salvation of souls and the reviving of saints are too important not to exercise faith and vision in the promotion of the upcoming crusade.

Following are many thought-provoking questions to assist in the involvement of people before and during the planned crusade:

* When should Sunday school teachers, youth leaders, and men and women's directors begin promoting the future evangelistic event?
* Who are the retired persons and others with surplus time in the congregation? Which ones would be willing to extend a personal invitation to church members and adherents by phone?
* Who was saved, baptized in the Holy Spirit, or healed in a past crusade? Would several of them be willing to

testify before the whole congregation in advance of this crusade?

* Is it possible to have a children's crusade in conjunction with this event for the adults?
* Can the ushers be rotated nightly to involve more participants in the crusade?
* Can the choir sing each evening?
* Is it possible to have ensembles and other special music throughout the crusade?
* Who is unable to drive during the evening hours due to physical limitations or lack of transportation? Can transportation be arranged for them?
* How many nursery and altar workers will be needed during the crusade?
* How can most church members be trained to invite their families and friends to the crusade?
* Should there be a different emphasis each night?
* How many sermons should the pastor preach on evangelism, discipleship, and revival prior to the crusade?
* Will the evangelist have adequate time on the opening day of the crusade to also promote the outreach, preach the gospel, and conduct an altar service?
* What time will the evening services begin and conclude?

The evangelist and the pastor must promote for the participation of the body of Christ and for the evangelization of the unchurched. W. E. Biederwolf said:

> The devil comes along with something the natural man wants, and he paints the town red to let them know he is coming. The church comes along with something the natural man doesn't want,

and thousands of pastors seem to think a mere announcement of the project from the pulpit is quite enough (Sweeting, 19).

Pray for Power

The tragedy of the twentieth-century church is not unanswered prayer but unoffered prayer. Although people, procedures, and programs are important while preparing for the evangelistic event, prayer is the greatest of all priorities. We cannot organize prayer, but we can organize opportunities for prayer. Be creative in arranging as many people as possible to pray specifically for the crusade. The pastor and the evangelist must be the pacesetters for the church in the area of prayer. Some possibilities of organizing people to pray are (1) Sunday school teachers turning their classes into prayer meetings on the opening day of the crusade, (2) arranging for church leaders to have church members in their same zip code area in their homes for prayer, (3) having various groups of people pray for the specific needs of salvation, healing, Holy Spirit baptism, etc., before the crusade, and (4) developing a twenty-four-hour prayer chain for the entire week prior to the crusade, involving as many as possible from the congregation.

It has been said, "Methods are many, principles are few; methods often change, but principles never do." The principle of prayer is foundational to success in crusade evangelism. Prayer will release the power of God and will motivate church members to be involved in other areas of the crusade as well. We must pray as though the outcome of the crusade depended on God and plan, prepare, and promote as though the results depended on us.

Provide for Preservation

The final invitation of the crusade is the conclusion of the event but only the beginning of the discipleship process of the new converts. Just as every believer needs to be involved in preparation for the gift of the evangelist to be exercised during the actual crusade, so must they fulfill their part in making disciples. The follow-up of newcomers is just as important as their initial response to the evangelist's salvation invitation. The ultimate purpose for ministry is not to make decisions but to make disciples (Matt. 28:18–20).

In the Great Commission, there is only one main Greek verb. It is "make disciples" *(mathēteúsate)*. The other verbs are participles. In the Greek text, participles depend on the main verb, thus everything in the Great Commission hinges on "make disciples." The goal of all evangelism efforts is discipleship. Only disciples can make disciples.

Evangelists should ask the pastors of upcoming crusades about the disciple-making process in their church. Ask if water baptism will take place during the crusade. If not, ascertain specifically when that will happen for new converts. Evangelists are just as responsible as the pastor for incorporating new converts into the body of Christ. Have you prepared a new convert's booklet, audiocassette, or video for those who respond to the altar invitation? If so, send a copy to the pastor prior to the crusade. Ask the pastor to review the material and to acknowledge acceptance or nonacceptance of it. Respect the pastor's answer.

If you have not prepared new convert materials, consider preparing them in the future. Examples of these kinds of materials can be obtained from other evangelists and pastors. When evangelists provide follow-up materials, they are helping to lead pastors and local churches in the disciple-making process.

I have come to the conclusion that if the pastor and the evangelist do not put the "big rocks" of evangelism and discipleship in first before the crusade ever begins, then there will not be enough time to do so during the local church crusade. I close this chapter with an illustration to help the reader understand the importance of starting crusade preparations far in advance.

> # Your ultimate purpose is not to make decisions but to make disciples.

Imagine a long table with a very large, open-mouthed jar sitting in the middle of it. There are various sizes of rocks on the table and a number of people around the table. These people are from the local church. An instructor is at the table in front of the open-mouthed jar. The instructor asks the people to do their best to put as many rocks into the jar as possible. The people begin to manipulate the rocks and put them into the jar. Someone says, "Oh, you can move one over this way and we can get another in over here."

Finally the jar appears to be as full as possible with rocks. The instructor asks those around the table, "Is the jar full?" They all answer in the affirmative. The instructor then reaches under the table and pulls out a box of pebbles. The eyes of all begin to widen as they watch the instructor pour the pebbles into the open-mouthed jar. The pebbles make their way in between the larger rocks in the jar. The jar now appears to be full.

Again, the instructor asks, "Is the jar now full?" This time the people respond, "As far as we can tell, the jar is now completely full." The instructor reaches down again and pulls out a box of sand. The people begin to laugh because they know what he was going to do. The tiny grains of sand fill the crevices and cracks in between the pebbles and the big rocks.

Then the instructor questions, "Now is the jar full?" They all respond, "As far as we can tell, it is as full as you can get it." The instructor then smiles and said, "I have one more thing I want to put in the jar." Picking up a pitcher of water, he pours water until the jar is full to the brim.

Finally the instructor asks, "What is the greatest lesson we can learn from this illustration?" Everyone agrees that "the most important lesson is that you have to put the big rocks in first. If you were to put the sand, the pebbles, or the water in first you would never get all the big rocks in."

This story is relevant for evangelism in the local church and for revival campaigns. Often, our lack of effectiveness in evangelism is thwarted because little things in ministry take all the time away from the most important things, which are evangelism and discipleship. This is the difference between the busyness of evangelism and the business of evangelism. If the big rocks of purpose, participation, personal relationships, preparation, prayer, promotion, presentation, and preservation are not put into their proper place before the crusade begins, then the evangelist and the pastor have chosen to limit their success in the upcoming evangelistic or revival crusade.

Evangelism Exercises

1. What are the six major steps to preparing for an upcoming crusade? Describe each step.
2. How can you be more creative in your crusade preparations?
3. In light of the big rocks story, what are some specific items that are causing you not to be able to get all the big rocks in for an upcoming crusade? Think about all areas of private and public life.

12

The Pentecostal Baptism and the Evangelist

Do you want to be a normal evangelist or an average evangelist? The normal evangelist is found in the New Testament; the average evangelist is often found today. Do you want to be a river or a reservoir? Do you want the Holy Spirit to flow through you and your ministry or do you want to contain the Holy Spirit all for yourself? Your answers to these questions will determine whether God will use you to lead Christians into Holy Spirit baptism.

Fifty days after the death of Jesus Christ, a tidal wave of Pentecost hit Jerusalem. Philip, the evangelist, not only led the Church in evangelism but also surfed the mighty wave of Pentecost to the Samaritans (see Acts 8). The Samaritans received the Holy Spirit and God confirmed the work of the evangelist with signs following the preaching of the Word. What kind of spiritual awakening is needed in our nation? What do our cities need today? Our cities need a Samaritan Pentecost.

Can there be any doubt that evangelists and Pentecost go hand-in-hand for the purposes of winning the lost to Christ and establishing local churches? Evangelists must lead the church into evangelism and new converts into the infilling of the Holy Spirit. What is the baptism in the Holy Spirit? How can evangelists lead Christians into the baptism of the Holy Spirit? According to the Jerusalem Pentecost (Acts 2), there are six biblical steps to leading the Church in general and Christians in particular into the baptism of the Holy Spirit.

Stand on the Scriptures

Our text states, "When the day of Pentecost had come . . ." (Acts 2:1). The day of Pentecost had come and gone more than 1,500 times since Moses instituted the feast 50 days after the Passover. On this occasion, however, Pentecost had come to stay. It can now be a spiritual norm for Christians to experience Pentecost every day of their lives.

What was the first New Testament Church's secret of success? How did they accomplish so much for God with so few evangelism tools at their disposal? How could Peter preach one message on the day of Pentecost to a hostile crowd and see three thousand souls saved?

The Early Church did not have big buildings, large budgets, and colorful billboards. The first-century Christians did not have television and radio stations, newspapers, magazines, printing presses, e-mail, fax machines, computers, the Internet, or other advances in technology. Yet, they turned their cities upside down, inside out, and right side up for the glory of God! Their successful soul-winning was accomplished through the power of the Holy Spirit.

Evangelists and pastors must *stand upon the Scriptures* and claim Pentecost for entire cities and individual churches. Joel predicted Pentecost (Joel 2:28–32). John preached about Pentecost (Matt. 3:11; Mark 1:8; Luke 3:16). Jesus promised Pentecost (Mark 16:17; Luke 24:49; Acts 1:4,5).

Evangelists and pastors must believe as Peter did: "This promise is for you and your children, and for all who are far off, as many as the Lord our God shall call to Himself" (Acts 2:39). Peter said the Holy Spirit is a *promised* gift ("this promise"), a *personal* gift ("for you"), a *parental* gift ("for your children"), a *provided* gift ("for all who are far off"), and a *providential* gift ("as many as the Lord our God shall call to Himself"). Pentecostal evangelists must preach on the subject of the baptism in the Holy Spirit and like Peter encourage people to receive the gift of the Holy Spirit for themselves.

Study the Saints

The early Christians illustrate several patterns for us to practice in order to experience Pentecost today. The first pattern is *obedience* (Acts 1:12). The apostle Paul indicates that approximately five hundred people saw Jesus leave Mount Olivet to return to His heavenly Father (1 Cor. 15:6). Just prior to His ascension, Jesus commanded His followers "not to leave Jerusalem, but to wait for what the Father had promised . . . for John truly baptized with water, but you shall be baptized with the Holy Spirit not many days from now" (Acts 1:4–5).

After Jesus departed for heaven, approximately 120 followers returned to Jerusalem (Acts 1:12, 15). Even though some five hundred people were given the command to go to Jerusalem, only a fourth of them obeyed. Those who obeyed Christ were baptized in the Holy Spirit. Obedience is necessary for a personal Pentecost. Evangelists, pastors, and congregations who determine to obey the commands of Christ will experience Pentecost in their crusades and local churches.

The second pattern for Pentecost is *openness* (Acts 1:14). Once the disciples returned to Jerusalem, they were "continually devoting themselves to prayer." Prayer opens hearts for the infilling of the Holy Spirit. Both evangelists and pastors should encourage and exemplify prayer for people to be baptized in the Holy Spirit. They should call special times of prayer during their crusades for the promise of Pentecost to be fulfilled during the nightly services.

Evangelists and pastors should encourage Christians to be open to the Holy Spirit during the altar service. Believers should be instructed to forget about other people around them and focus on Christ above them. Moreover, they need to be motivated to pray for the promise of the baptism in the Holy Spirit to be fulfilled in each life around the altar area. Other Spirit-filled Christians should also be led to pray for those seeking the baptism in the Holy Spirit.

> **Evangelists and pastors must believe as Peter did: This promise is for all.**

The third pattern for Pentecost is *oneness* (Acts 1:14; 2:1). The early Christians had a singleness of purpose.

Disunity hinders Pentecostal revival. The evangelist should encourage people to get right with each other and with God. Each must forgive the other so that revival will come to their church. Furthermore, the evangelist is to exemplify unity with the pastor before the entire congregation.

Sense the Sound

The Bible states, "Suddenly there came from heaven a noise like a violent, rushing wind, and it filled the whole house where they were sitting" (Acts 2:2). The Holy Spirit is symbolized by wind. In both the Old and New Testaments, the word for "wind" is the same as for "Spirit." If evangelists and pastors are going to lead churches when the "wind of the Spirit" is moving, they must understand the dynamics of wind.

First, wind is *invisible*. No one has ever taken a picture of the wind. An individual can see only the effects of the wind. In like manner, even though the Holy Spirit is invisible, the effects of the Holy Spirit will be evident for the evangelist and pastor and the church to see. When the wind of the Spirit is moving, there will be liberty in the worship service. People will be convicted of sin and will accept Christ as Savior. Others will be healed of sicknesses. Christians will receive the baptism of the Holy Spirit. Saints will become soul-winners. Demonic powers will be defeated. People will experience deliverance.

Evangelists and pastors must recognize the outward signs of the moving of the Holy Spirit. They need to learn to see the invisible through the visible. They need to allow the unseen Holy Spirit to guide throughout the crusade service.

Second, the wind is *irresistible*. No one can capture the

wind. A person cannot grasp a fistful of wind on a windy day or fill a large container with wind. Jesus said the Holy Spirit is like the wind (John 3:8). The wind of the Spirit blows wherever it wants to go.

The evangelist and pastor cannot always predict the way or ways the wind of the Spirit will move during a service. The itinerant preacher must depend on the leading of the Spirit. This dependence brings excitement in evangelism. Do you want to minister where the Holy Spirit is going in the twenty-first century? Instead of praying for God to bless what you are doing, discover what God is blessing and get involved in it for His glory!

Third, the wind is *indispensable.* Life on this earth cannot exist without wind. Wind determines our weather patterns. The local church cannot live without the wind of the Holy Spirit. If the wind of the Holy Spirit is taken from the church, then formalism and rituals will be left for the people. Dead religions deserve a proper burial. The local church does not gather to mourn a corpse but to worship a resurrected Savior!

See the Sign

On the Day of Pentecost, the Holy Spirit was also symbolized by fire (Acts 2:3). Why is the Holy Spirit symbolized by fire?

First, fire *cleanses.* It purifies. When Christians walk in the Spirit, they will not fulfill the works of the flesh (Gal. 5:18). The evangelist and pastor must live consecrated lives. This kind of lifestyle is possible only through the work of the Holy Spirit.

Second, fire *consumes*. Fire does not distinguish between one object and another. Fire consumes everything in its path. On the Day of Pentecost there was wind and fire. Every time wind and fire get together, something big happens. People will gather to watch a raging fire.

Would you like your ministry to be consumed and controlled by the Holy Spirit?

Do you desire for the fire of the Holy Spirit to consume every area of your life? Would you like for your evangelistic or pastoral ministry to be consumed and controlled by the Holy Spirit? Do you know the difference between being filled with and being full of the Holy Spirit? Just as Jesus (Luke 4:1), Stephen (Acts 6 and 7), and Barnabas (Acts 11:19–26) were full of the Holy Spirit, anyone can be full of the Holy Spirit today.

Third, fire *causes* fire. When there is fire and wind, it will be likely to spread. This principle is also true in evangelism. If the fire burns within the evangelist or pastor or both, soon the local church will be on fire. If an entire church is on fire for God, the community or city will soon feel the effects of revival fire.

Do not be overly concerned about wildfire; there is always some wildfire associated with a raging fire. Just do not become an instrument of wildfire. Lead the congregation in true, biblical revival, not emotionalism. Maintain balance in your evangelism. Make sure the wind of the Spirit is spreading the revival fire and not the vain imaginations of people. My personal belief is that it is easier to constrain a fanatic than to resurrect a corpse!

Speak with the Spirit

Some denominations teach that the gifts of the Holy Spirit ceased when the Apostles died; however, there is no scriptural support for this conclusion. Others teach that the responsible interpreter of Scripture derives doctrine only from the Epistles and not from the Book of Acts (Fee, Dunn, and others). However, doctrines concerning the nature of God are rooted mostly in Old Testament narratives, and Paul said that, "All scripture is inspired by God and profitable for teaching" (2 Tim. 3:16). It is incongruent to teach that the Bible is relevant for today and then dichotomize it into irrelevancy. The Bible states: "They were all filled with the Holy Spirit and began to speak with other tongues, as the Spirit was giving them utterance" (Acts 2:4; 10:44–48; 19:1–7).

If evangelists and pastors want to lead people into the baptism in the Holy Spirit, they need to comprehend the three biblical phases of Spirit-baptism. First, Christians are to be encouraged to *receive the Spirit* (v. 4a). God's will is for "all" to be filled with the Spirit. Evangelists need not hurry the altar service. Some people instantly receive the Spirit while others need more time during the altar service.

Second, evangelists and pastors should instruct people to *respond to the Spirit* (v. 4b). The Bible states: "they . . . began to speak with other tongues." This is where the rubber meets the road in contemporary charismatic theology. What is meant by "other tongues"? The term for "tongues" means "languages." These languages can be known to other people (Acts 2:5–11) and at times can be known only to heaven (1 Cor. 14:2,28). These "tongues" are not merely gibberish or ecstatic speech. On the Day of Pentecost, the disciples spoke "unlearned" languages but not "unknown" languages. These languages were an external evidence of an internal experience.

Who should speak with "other tongues"? All Christians should strive to be baptized with the Holy Spirit. The apostle Paul "preserved the practice" of speaking in "tongues through correction" and did not "prohibit it by condemnation" (1 Cor. 13–15) (Hayford, 17). He indicated all Christians did not speak in tongues (1 Cor. 12:30) but he wished that they did (1 Cor. 14:5). The baptism in the Holy Spirit, with the external evidence of speaking in other tongues, is for every Christian.

Though not all Christians spoke in tongues, Paul wished they did.

Why do some Christians fail to speak in other tongues? When a Christian speaks in tongues, the language is not understood by the mind (1 Cor. 14:15). The mind understands natural language because it has been learned. However, it is not natural for a person to speak a language he or she has not learned or does not understand with the mind. The baptism in the Holy Spirit is the reverse of the natural way of speaking a language. Instead of speaking what is first understood, Christians speak first what is not understood by the mind. This is one aspect of the supernatural work of the Holy Spirit.

Who does the speaking? Many well-meaning Christians are afraid they may be "doing" the speaking in tongues. Thus, they clam up and fail to receive fully the gift of the Holy Spirit. On the Day of Pentecost, the disciples began to speak in other tongues. They spoke for themselves. No one can speak for someone else. The person who is filled with the Holy Spirit does "do" the speaking in tongues. Who else could do the speaking? If a person waits until there is full understanding about the baptism in the Holy Spirit, that same individual might never be baptized in the Holy Spirit.

Did you know Mary, the mother of Jesus, spoke in other tongues? She was present in the Upper Room on the day of Pentecost (Acts 1:12–14). If it is all right for Mary, then it is all right for us today! Jesus said his disciples would speak with new tongues (Mark 16:17). Therefore, all Christians should desire to receive and respond to the Holy Spirit.

Third, the evangelist and pastor should teach the people to *rely on the Spirit* (v. 4c). On the Day of Pentecost, the disciples spoke in tongues "as the Spirit was giving them utterance." They continued to speak in other languages as the Spirit enabled them. They spoke a new language through the Holy Spirit. Here is the picture of people welcoming the Holy Spirit and the Holy Spirit working with the people. When the Spirit creates an utterance, the person must be willing to speak forth that utterance for Baptism to be complete.

In light of the above teaching regarding the baptism in the Holy Spirit, ministers should not manipulate or coerce Christians into the Spirit-baptism. Christians should not be told what to say. Allow the Holy Spirit to speak through them.

Furthermore, Pentecostal evangelists and pastors need to resist being carried away by "third wave" Pentecostalism. At the beginning of the twentieth century, the first wave of Pentecostalism was summarized simply by, "You *must* speak in tongues." The second wave of Pentecostalism during the middle of the twentieth century was summarized by "You *may* speak in tongues." Some in the third wave of Pentecostalism summarize it as "You *may not* speak in tongues." Instead of going from you "must" to you "may not," the Pentecostal church needs a fresh outpouring of the Holy Spirit. Evangelists should motivate Christians to move from being non-Pentecostal and part-time Pentecostal to being full-time Pentecostal!

Step Out in Service

What is the purpose of the baptism in the Holy Spirit? On the Day of Pentecost, Christians went from "sitting" (v. 2) to "standing" (v. 14). The purpose of Pentecost is to help the Church move from its seat to its feet! The power of the Spirit will help the Church to go from weakness to witness and will turn saints into soul-winners.

Evangelists and pastors must teach and preach in such a manner as to illicit an appropriate response regarding Spirit-baptism. On the Day of Pentecost some people were *amazed* by the work of the Spirit (Acts 2:12), others were *amused* by the work of the Holy Spirit (Acts 2:14), yet many people *accepted* the work of the Holy Spirit (Acts 2:37). Just like Peter taught from Scripture about the infilling of the Spirit, the minister needs to explain biblically the gift of the Spirit to the congregation.

Not everyone will believe and receive the blessed gift of the Spirit; nevertheless, evangelists must preach Jesus Christ as Savior and be prepared for signs to follow the message. Pray that people will ask, "What does this mean?" (Acts 2:14). Then communicate the gospel in such a manner that people will ask, "What shall we do?" (Acts 2:37). Unless people ask these two questions, they will not be saved or baptized in the Holy Spirit. Just as the waves of the ocean make their way to the shore, the waves of Pentecostal revival can make their way to a nation. Evangelists and pastors must keep the big picture of revival in sight. Never forget the principle of the ebb and flow of the waves of revival. James Burns states:

> Any progress (that moves us closer in our relationship toward God) is like the incoming tide. Each wave is revival, going forward, receding, and being followed by another. To the onlooker it seems as if nothing is gained, but the force behind the ebb and flow is the power of the tide (Burns, 14).

Since the last Great Spiritual Awakening of 1857–59 in America, the next wave of revival has been building, churning, and making its way to our shores. Be patient. Be ready. Look for the next wave of Pentecostal revival to come to America. "As much as human nature creates an undertow that drags us down, God responds by moving us forward" (Phillips, 209). It is the power of the unseen spiritual tide.

As the wave of Pentecostal revival moves closer, its crest will eventually be seen. Just as the wave does not last long, the wave of the next Pentecostal revival will be brief compared to overall history. Yet, the effects of true, life-changing Pentecostal revival can last for generations.

As the wave of Spirit-filled revival increases in strength, evangelists and pastors must be ready to surf this tide of spiritual awakening. Evangelists will have opportunities to lead the Church in revival and cities into spiritual awakenings. However, the time span will be brief. Evangelists will either see the front side of the wave in evangelism or the back side of missed opportunities. Do not underestimate the force behind the incoming tide. The same "law (or principle) which moves the mighty tides of the ocean is the same which ruffles the surface of the little pool made by rain on a summer afternoon" (Burns, 14). Align yourself to catch the incoming wave of Pentecostal revival.

Evangelism Exercises

1. Have you been baptized in the Holy Spirit? If so, how do know you have been baptized in the Spirit?
2. What are the steps to leading a local church or Christians into Spirit-baptism? Summarize.
3. What is meant by "third-wave" charismatic theology?
4. What is the "ebb and flow" of revival?

13

The Preaching of the Evangelist

If the minister will assume the responsibility of filling the pulpit, God will take care of filling the building. "We must make sure that our evangelism does not draw upon a bag of clever tricks. . . . The Church must slay all tricks, traps, and techniques which will cheapen evangelism" (Autrey, 16). How does a preacher go about "filling the pulpit" on a weekly basis for effective evangelism? It is important both for the experienced and inexperienced minister to correctly understand New Testament evangelistic preaching. It is imperative for the biblical preacher to cross the bridge of the ancient, unindustrialized past to the computerized age of the present. A well-balanced philosophy of evangelistic sermon preparation is the key to unlocking yesterday's biblical principles in order to transform them into timeless truths for today. This sermonic philosophy of preaching is dependent upon the anointing of the Holy Spirit to make ultimately an eternal difference in the hearts of the listeners. Biblical, evangelistic preaching is Holy Spirit empowered, authoritatively proclaimed, and has contemporary application of the entire Word of God for the purposes of equipping the saints and evangelizing the lost. Above all else, the minister is called to preach Christ to the Church and the world.

The Picture of Evangelistic Preaching

Incarnation is the picture of evangelistic preaching. This has to do with what evangelists in particular and ministers in general believe the "inspiration of Scripture" is composed of in our day. The Bible was written not to put the lives of people into print but to put life into the souls of people. Incarnation depends on inspiration. A person cannot have "the Word become flesh" without "breath." The term *inspiration* means "breath." "For no prophecy was ever made by an act of human will, but men moved by the Holy Spirit spoke from God" (2 Pet. 1:21). "All Scripture is inspired by God" (2 Tim. 3:16), or given by the breath of God.

In essence, the Bible was brought about by God breathing the words on the page. By His Spirit, God was quickening the authors of the Bible to write His words for us. The breath of God moved upon them and through them in a manner that caused them to write the words of God on paper. Thus, the words in the Bible got there from the breath of God and the hand of man.

The challenge evangelists and pastors face today is knowing how to "inhale" correctly *(exegesis)* the breath of God, that is, the Word of God. The goal is not just to get the Word of God into the minister's head but into the heart as well. This is where the role of the Holy Spirit comes in as it relates to evangelistic preaching. Do you know the difference between just speaking a sermon with your own breath and preaching the Word of God through the breath, or anointing, of God?

After ministers have inhaled the breath of God and His Word, they are to "exhale" the Word of God through anointed preaching so people can live again. The minister can either share the inspired Scriptures as information or for incarnation. Just as the Holy Spirit birthed (conceived) Jesus in Mary, anointed ministry births Jesus in the lives of others today.

Evangelistic preaching impregnates people with the seed (*sperma,* from which the term *sperm* is derived), the Word of God, and eternal life springs forth within their hearts. The result is salvation through belief in Jesus Christ. That is how the "Word becomes flesh" today. People must experience the new birth of Jesus inside them to enter into salvation.

The Purpose of Evangelistic Preaching

There is a fundamental difference in aim between a lecturer and a preacher. A lecturer explains a subject, a preacher seeks character change in the hearts and lives of the listeners. For example, a lecturer may explain botany, but an evangelist is to "raise flowers" (Brown, 5). Evangelists and pastors are called to present the gospel in such a manner that lives are forever changed.

The purpose of evangelistic preaching is to win the lost to Christ. The goal of a sermon is to persuade people. The main purpose of a sermon is not simply to exegete a text correctly but to produce godly character in people's lives.

The minister is not called by God to merely motivate the audience but also to activate them. Most often preaching does not fail because of logistics but because the preacher does not know the audience. People need their ears turned into eyes so they can see the truth (Perry, 166). If the evangelist or pastor preaches offensively, people will respond defensively. As a result of the sermon, the congregation should live out the principles that were proposed in the message.

The Precepts of Evangelistic Sermons

The precepts of evangelistic preaching are designed to be interwoven both during the private phase of study and the public phase of preaching the gospel. In essence, these six precepts build a theological and homiletical bridge between the purpose and preparations of evangelistic preaching. First, evangelistic preaching is *scriptural*. When an evangelist or a pastor causes people to read the Word of God, the Word of God reads them. The Word of God is "the power of God unto salvation" (Rom. 1:16), a source of faith (Rom. 10:17), a hammer that breaks (Jer. 23:29), and a sword that pierces (Heb. 4:12). God has promised to bless His Word (Isa. 55:10–11), not the stories of the minister. "God never puts a premium on an empty brain just because one has a full heart" (Perry, 162).

Second, evangelistic preaching is to be *salvational*. Jesus Christ should be the center of all gospel preaching. Christ is the center of both the Old and New Testaments (Larsen, 80). Effective, evangelistic preaching includes the doctrines of sin, the Cross, Resurrection, judgment, the holiness of God, hell, heaven, repentance, faith, and Jesus Christ as Savior.

Third, evangelistic preaching is *searching* (Autrey, 120). It begins where people are and leads them to where they need to be. It does not condemn. It convicts the conscience, challenges the brain, and convinces the soul. Someone has said, "You're never preaching until the audience hears Another voice."

Fourth, evangelistic preaching is *sympathetic*. The minister is to be positive and passionate. People need to see visions more than hear reasons.

Preaching usually fails not because of logistics but because of not knowing one's audience.

Fifth, evangelistic preaching is *simple* (Autrey, 120). It is more difficult to put great truths into simple, everyday language than to continue using "Christianese." In order for people to respond to the gospel, they must first understand it. A message that is simple to comprehend is evidence of hard work and much study.

Sixth, evangelistic preaching gives a *summons* (Larsen, 99). The invitation is the most important part of the evangelistic sermon (see pages 198–201). The invitation becomes the moral intersection, where people will turn right to Christ or the wrong direction leading to hell. "The opportunity for men to confess Christ now sends a signal from heaven that God accepts you now as you are" (Kendall, 25).

The Preparation for Evangelistic Preaching

There are eight steps to effective evangelistic preaching (see chart on pages 200–201), steps that can be applied to various kinds of sermons (e.g., topical, textual, expository). Because I believe the evangelist should strive to provide evangelistic expository preaching, I have designed this process with the expository sermon in mind. Expository preaching is

> [t]he communication of a biblical concept, derived from and transmitted through a historical, grammatical, and literary study of a passage in its context, which the Holy Spirit first applies to the personality and experience of the preacher, then through him to his hearers (Robinson, 20).

Each step builds upon the other, leading the evangelist and pastor upward to the pulpit.

INTERCESSION

The first step upward to the pulpit of proclamation is *intercession.* Of course, the preacher is to be a praying person every day, not just when evangelistic messages are being prepared for a crusade (see chapter 6). "He does not stop to pray: he simply does not stop from prayer" (Quayle, 261). Jesus did not teach His disciples how to preach but how to pray (Patterson, 155). Prayer should precede preparation and preaching; our focus here, however, is the role of prayer in the preparation of evangelistic messages. At every juncture in the sermonic preparation, a spirit of prayer should be in the evangelist's heart. Yet, today the emphasis is more on how to preach rather than how to pray in order to preach. This is a missing element in effective evangelistic preaching.

Pray over and through all the steps of preparation for effective evangelistic preaching. Pray for the lost who will attend your crusade. Ask the Lord to direct every thought during your sermon preparation for the purposes of connecting with, communicating to, and finally converting the lost to Christ.

The second step upward to the pulpit of proclamation is *interpretation.* For exegesis to produce a thorough biblical theology, the evangelist and pastor must have a high view of scriptural authority. Scripture must have the final authority in all aspects of evangelistic ministry. "If there is no difference between the Bible and Aesop's fables, or Joseph Smith's tablets, we are abandoned with a hopeless mixture of truth and error calculated to foster hesitation and equivocation in the pulpit" (Larsen, 25). Our view of the Bible will determine how we preach it in the pulpit.

The meaning of the passage is achievable when all the data is researched by the evangelist. Ministers must keep in mind they are not called to make the preaching text relevant but to show its relevance. If Scripture is not already relevant, then the most gifted preacher cannot make it so. It is self-defeating to advocate that it is the preacher's responsibility to make the text relevant to today (Greidanus, 157). Yet, how does an evangelist make the Bible relevant to the churched and unchurched? How do itinerants transfer a relevant message from Scripture to the present culture?

Historical-Cultural Research

The historical-cultural research focuses the sermonizer on the times and events of the original writer and then compels them forward to the present. To transfer the relevant message of the past to the present, the historical-cultural gap must be crossed. God's Word entered history in a relevant fashion; it can enter again our world today (Greidanus, 159). But the historical-cultural gap is not crossed by allegorizing, spiritualizing, and moralizing the preaching text, so can the horizons of past and present be merged to produce application for the listener?

Evangelists need to transfer consistently the specific message of a text and not simply its isolated parts (Greidanus, 166). Relevance is lost in a long didactic discourse on the details of the preaching passage. People want to hear the message of the passage. Before ministers can make proper application of Scripture, they must know what the original writer wanted to convey to his readers.

Grammatical-Syntactical Analysis

The grammatical-syntactical analysis will permit the preacher to trace the interrelationships of the parts of the passage for its meaning and will reveal the thrust of the message for the congregation. The diligent evangelist finds meaning as he or she connects words together in a sentence, paragraph, chapter, or book.

However, the total framework within which the biblical authors communicated and how that message relates to our own times is accomplished through grasping the whole before attempting to dissect the individual parts of a text.

All aspects of the "hermeneutical spiral" (see Figure 9, page 179) are interwoven for the purpose of creating relevant meaning (Osborne). It is the total message that contains propositional truth. The sermonizer needs to look beneath the "surface structure" of grammar, semantics, and syntax to the "deep structure"—the message behind the words. Richard Palmer writes, "To understand a text is to understand the question behind the text, the question that called the text into being" (Palmer, 250). Answering why the text was written is at the heart of interpretation in order to apply the text to the present situation.

The sermonizer must ask and answer seven questions during the interpretation process. (1) What does the text say? The evangelist or pastor should study different translations, analyze the grammar, and digest background materials. (2) How does the text say it? Determine the genre of literature. (3) What did the text mean? See the text through the eyes of the original author and his readers. (4) What does the text mean?

> **Answering why the text was written—the heart of interpretation.**

Attach a zip code to the text. (5) What does the text mean to me? The sermonizer must look through the eyes of the Holy Spirit for himself before preaching the gospel to others. (6) What does it mean to the congregation? Figuratively, gather the congregation around the study desk while applying the text to today's world. Anticipate objections. Turn resistance into readiness. (7) How can I make it meaningful to others? An evangelistic sermon becomes meaningful through godly creativity. Preachers must allow their imagination to turn their sermons into mirrors so people can see themselves in the light of truth.

Commentaries

Sermon preparation is more than parroting the commentator's ideas and conclusions. In most instances, commentaries should be consulted last, to test the minister's interpretations of the immediate passage. Evangelists and pastors should first study the text inductively to protect themselves from an uneducated reliance on commentaries. The commentator's evidence is then weighed carefully in light of the interpreter's exegesis of the immediate context. The context is kept in mind at every level of the hermeneutics spiral in order to proclaim a relevant biblical message.

A critical evaluation of one's presuppositions about the text is necessary because the minister brings church traditions, communal beliefs, and personal experiences to the text. The preacher must separate church traditions and dogma from Scripture. The personal experiences of evangelists and pastors within their own community of faith help shape their lives and worldview. Careful sermon preparation will stop the proclaimer of God's Word from reworking the intended meaning of the text to fit personal experiences or goals. A "hermeneutic of humility" must be applied when Scripture dictates that one's previous theological system or a church's doctrine needs modification or elimination. It is the continuous interaction between the text and the preacher's presuppositions that form an upward spiral to relevant truth.

Last, the interpreter "principalizes" meaning into timeless truths (Kaiser). The text sets the agenda for the sermon. Grammatical-syntactical exegesis and historical-cultural background of the text reshape the minister's presuppositions.

Hermeneutical Spiral

WHAT THE BIBLE MEANT THEN (PAST)
SURFACE (Exegesis)
SPIRITUAL PRINCIPLE (Theology)
IDENTIFY LIFE SITUATION
MEDITATION
PARALLELS FOR TODAY
GENERAL APPLICATION
SPECIFIC APPLICATION
WHAT THE BIBLE MEANS NOW (PRESENT)

Figure 9. The interpreter's hermeneutical spiral.

Between Two Worlds

Deductive and inductive reasoning are necessary to complete the bridge from an author's past meaning to relevant truth for today. Deductive study establishes the theological systems (overall doctrines) based on scriptural evidence.

Inductive study utilizes imagination to move the sermonizer from the theological systems to modern-day applications. An overlap between the past and present horizons is required for recontextualization (Stott). Lively preaching paints a picture for the listener's heart. It enables the audience to see the parallels between the biblical author's intended meaning and relevance for today. In summary, proper sermon preparation reveals past truth from the text, relates personal truth to the interpreter, and releases propositional truth for the congregation.

ILLUMINATION

The third step upward to the pulpit of proclamation is *illumination.* The unseen spiritual world is just as resourceful, if not more so, than the seen world of exegetical exactitude in the minister's office. The same Holy Spirit who moved on the apostles and prophets of old desires to illuminate our minds today. In John MacArthur's opinion:

> No clear understanding of Scripture leading to powerful preaching is possible without the Spirit's work of illumination . . . Powerful preaching occurs only when a Spirit-illumined man of God expounds clearly and compellingly God's Spirit-inspired revelation in Scripture to a Spirit-illumined congregation (MacArthur, 102–03).

There is a difference between inspiration and illumination. Inspiration is the process by which men "inscripturated" the revelation of God (MacArthur, 105). The apostle Paul needed inspiration in order to write the revelation of God (things previously unknown). While inspiration was the needed vehicle to reveal eternal truth from God to us in the Bible, illumination is needed today to fully ascertain the correct interpretation and application of a particular pericope. The anointing, or illumination, of the Holy Spirit teaches the meaning of the Word of God (1 John 2:20,27). The Word of God comes alive for the sermonizer when illumination becomes a part of his or her preparation. Henry C. Fish warns:

> A sermon may be constructed after the best models; it may conform to all the rules of homiletics; the text may be suitable and fruitful; the plan may be faultless; the execution may discover genius and judgment; there may be accurate analysis and strong reasoning; proof and motive; solidarity and beauty; logic and persuasion; argument direct and indirect; perspicuity, purity, correctness, propriety, precision; description, antithesis, metaphor, allegory, comparison; motives from goodness, motives from happiness, motives from self-love; appeals to the sense of the beautiful, the sense of right, to the affections, the passions, the emotions; a sermon may be all this, and yet that very sermon, even though it fell from the lips of a prince of pulpit oratory, were as powerless in the renewal of a soul as in raising the dead, if unaccompanied by the omnipotent energy of the Holy Spirit (Perry, 167).

IMAGINATION

The fourth step upward to the pulpit of proclamation is *imagination.* Imagination is the bridge between the ancient past and the contemporary present. There is a vast difference between fantasy and imagination. A former doctoral professor of mine, Warren Wiersbe, once likened fantasy to Disney World and imagination to Epcot Center. Disney World causes one to escape the real world while Epcot causes one to enter a brand new world. Evangelists and pastors are to preach the gospel in such a way as to help people see a new world with Christ in the center. One of the reasons the great entertainment centers of the world can charge exorbitant prices and still turn away thousands of people is creativity. The reason so many people sit sanctimoniously in our sanctuaries half asleep is because ministers often do and say the same things, the same way while expecting a miracle on Sunday. Our culture demands creativity!

Effective speakers understand how listeners view their world.

The humorist was correct when he said, "Insanity is doing the same thing, the same old way, expecting different results." As evangelists, we must not fail to use our God-given imaginations to discover creative techniques for maturing the saints and reaching our cities.

Evangelists and pastors need to remember that they do not see the world as other people see it but as they themselves see it. "We assume that the world is the way we speak it, that reality matches the 'metaphors we live by'" (Troeger, 120). Effective communicators understand how listeners imagine or view their world. The sacred responsibility of the sermonizer is to use biblically guided imagination to cross the bridge from the past to the present. The hazard lies in the fact that the preacher's mind serves as a "filter" or paradigm for accurately bringing the sacred message of the scriptural passage into the arena of ideas today.

"Imagination is the imaging function of the mind. It is thinking by seeing, as contrasted with reasoning" (Broadus, 221). Imagination puts flesh and clothes on mere naked ideas and facts. It makes the unknown known and the unseen seen. Warren Wiersbe astutely declares:

> "Imagineering" a text means trying to see it in a contemporary setting and identifying in it images that speak to people today. We must take care, though, in presenting this contemporary image . . . that we don't abandon the original image or alter it to suit our purposes, because we're preaching God's Word and not our own ideas. The modern equivalent is the point of contact for the text and never a substitute (Wiersbe, 286–87).

The imaginative mind sees how different facts and ideas can be brought together to build a sermon. Just as a contractor knows how to pull together blueprints, brick, sand, and wood to build a house, the creative sermonizer knows how to tie together the parts of exegesis to form a meaning and the aspects of homiletics to form a message. The creative preacher builds his or her other message, word by word, to form sentences that picture eternal truth for the modern mind. Imagination arouses faith in God and His Word. Imagination makes history come alive. Imagination is one of the strongest allies of the minister to change lives forever.

Imagination also helps the evangelist and pastor to get into the lives of people. For example, if ministers get into the lives of young people, they will have the attention of young people. If ministers get into the lives of a lot of different kinds of people, many different kinds of people will come to hear them.

Words are outward expressions of thoughts within in a person's mind. Creativity and imagination can make thoughts visible. We cannot see the thoughts of God. They are hidden from us. But God revealed those thoughts through the life of Jesus. Jesus became both the outward visual and vocal expressions of the hidden thoughts of God. We should strive to help people who are blind to the truths and thoughts of God in His Word to see visions in their minds and the difference Jesus Christ will make in their life.

Creativity is the product of imagination. Wiersbe has profoundly written:

> Creativity is the result of the imagination bringing together both science and art and allowing them to interact. Creativity is both left-brain and right-brain, both analysis and synthesis. Analysis deals with facts and concepts, synthesis with truths and pictures. The scientist in you takes the text apart (exegesis) and the poet in you puts it back together (homiletics) so that concepts become pictures and information becomes motivation (Wiersbe, 292).

Imagination and creativity are to be used all along the way of sermon preparation. Just like prayer keeps the sermonizer in tune with God, imagination and creativity will keep the sermonizer relevant to the world. To be effective communicators of the gospel, preachers must stay in touch with the eternal world of God, the temporary world of nature and humanity, the pragmatic world within the body, mind, and spirit, and the life-changing world of the Bible (Wiersbe, 297). The imaginative sermonizer has the distinct ability to pull all of these worlds together into an effective preaching ministry.

Every evangelistic message must be packaged in some

creative way in order for the audience to grasp its meaning and to be motivated by it. The biblical text determines the substance of the sermon. The preacher determines the structure of the sermon. As Rick Warren notes, "The crowd does not determine whether or not you speak the truth: The truth is not optional. But your audience does determine which truths you choose to speak about" (Warren, 228). Even though this book will not include an extended discussion of homiletics, the imaginative process is crystallized through the homiletic skills of the minister. Homiletics pulls all of the data together. The diagram below illustrates the differences between preparation and packaging of the sermon.

PREPARATION OF SERMON	PACKAGING OF SERMON
FACTS	TRUTHS
PAST EVENTS	PRESENT EXPERIENCES
DATED HISTORY	TIMELESS TRUTHS
THE TEXT	THE TIMES
INTERPRETATION	APPLICATION
ORDER OF PASSAGE	NOT NECESSARILY ORDER OF THE PASSAGE
INCLUDES ALL MATERIAL	SELECTIVE
NOT UNIFIED	MUST BE UNIFIED

Figure 10. Differences between the preparation and packaging of a sermon.

There are at least eight thought-provoking questions for the sermonizer to ask during the packaging of the effective evangelistic message: (1) To whom will I be preaching (1 Cor. 9:22–23)? (2) What does the passage say about their needs (Luke 4:18–19; 2 Tim. 3:16)? (3) What is the most practical way to say it (James 1:22; Titus 2:1)? Give specific actions. Show them how to do it. Think zip code. (4) What is the most positive way to say it (Prov. 16:21; Col. 4:5-6)? (5) What is the most encouraging way to say it (Prov. 12:25; Rom. 15:4)? (6) What is the simplest way to say it (1 Cor. 2:1; 2:4)?

To be relevant in a secular society, these three questions must be answered . . .

(Simple does not mean shallow.) Avoid using religious terms. Keep your outline simple. Write your sermon into a single sentence. Prepare your sermon outline in the present tense. (7) What is the most personal way to say it (2 Cor. 6:11; 1 Thess. 2:8)? (8) What is the most interesting way to say it (Col. 4:5–6)? (See "The Presentation of Evangelistic Preaching," 201–204 ff.) For the contemporary minister to be relevant in a secular society, there are three all-encompassing questions that must be answered before presenting the gospel today. These three questions summarize this entire section on the preparation of evangelistic preaching:

(1) What is the point of the passage? This is accomplished

through investigation and interpretation by the preacher. (2) What are the pictures for the people? Creativity and imagination build the bridge from the ancient text to the present day. (3) What is the package for the preacher? The preacher will have to decide, based on his audience, exactly how the sermon is to be structured for maximum results.

ILLUSTRATIONS

The fifth step upward to the pulpit of proclamation is *illustrations*. Just as the Holy Spirit illuminates the mind during the exegesis phase, illustrations paint pictures in the minds of the listeners during the preaching phase. Illustrations are not to be a substitute for solid scriptural substance; they are to illustrate various truths or principles throughout the evangelistic message. Illustrations allow the audience time to catch their breath mentally before diving down again for deep truth. Learn to use illustrations at the right time and the right place during a sermon to reach the maximum impact in the listeners' hearts. Stories stir the emotions, open the mind, paint pictures, help the memory, and keep one's attention. Have a variety of illustrations in each sermon.

Timely illustrations can be found in books, magazines, newspapers, conversations, television programs, technology, the arts and sciences, sports—most arenas of life. Look for them, listen for them, think about them, file them. And by all means cultivate them: Practice them before preaching them.

Everyone likes to hear a good story. Illustrations are the spices that awaken the five senses of a person and make the sermon easier to swallow mentally, emotionally, psychologically, and spiritually.

INTRODUCTION

The sixth step upward to the pulpit of proclamation is the *introduction*. When does the introduction begin? People are sizing up the minister before he or she enters the pulpit. They are judging sincerity, integrity, mannerisms, and believability. The experienced preacher knows that the audience is watching during praise and worship, special singing, and the offering times. It is extremely important for the evangelist or pastor to set the tone of the message long before the actual sermon.

What are the qualities of a good introduction? Haddon Robinson has clearly described the qualities required for an introduction. These qualities are (1) commands attention, (2) surfaces needs, and (3) introduces the body of the sermon (Robinson, 160–65). He summarized the required length of an introduction with the following:

> The introduction needs to be long enough to capture attention, needs, and orient the audience to the subject, the idea, and the first point. Until this is done, the introduction is incomplete, after that the introduction is too long (Robinson, 165).

There are nearly limitless ways to begin an introduction. The speaker can use an illustration, statistics, rhetorical questions, a paradoxical statement, a song, the scriptural passage, humor, authoritative quotations, and many others. The speaker should view the introduction "not in terms of what begins your presentation but in terms of what will open up the audience" (Arredondo, 36).

How can you know what kind of introduction is appropriate for the evangelistic message? The best introduction satisfies all three of the following questions: "What's the most relevant way to your subject and to the audience? What's most appropriate to the setting? What best suits your own personal style, so you can begin comfortably and naturally?" (Arrendondo, 40). Do not underestimate the impact of a powerful introduction. Remember, "the first ninety seconds of any presentation are crucial" (Hoff, 30). If the evangelist or pastor does not capture the attention of the congregation at the very beginning of the sermon, then the audience may never enter into the heart and soul of the sermon.

IMPARTATION

It is possible to examine exegetically the speeches and sermons of the New Testament, asking a variety of questions relating to evangelistic preaching. Who is the finest evangelist in the New Testament? Who connected and communicated with his audience more effectively than any other New Testament evangelist?

Jesus Christ served as a Spirit-filled evangelist in the New Testament era. Even though one could argue that John the Baptist served as an evangelist in the New Testament era, Jesus described John as the greatest of all the "prophets" (Matt. 11:7–15; Luke 7:26–28). Jesus followed the twofold ministry tracks of evangelizing the lost and equipping the saints in Ephesians 4:11–16. Christ trained leaders for the purpose of evangelism. He was not only the great physician, the master teacher, and the suffering servant but also "the excellent evangelist." He epitomizes the evangelist's paradigm for culturally-relevant, Spirit-empowered, Bible-based, evangelistic preaching that produces changed lives.

Jesus was a master communicator. There are at least five corollaries of communication found in the effective evangelistic preaching ministry of Jesus Christ. He inductively and deductively combined the text with His times for the dual purposes of evangelizing the lost and equipping His disciples. For ministers to be more effective in the twenty-first century, they need to compare and contrast their preaching ministry to the first-century evangelistic preaching ministry of Jesus.

It is possible to study the spirit, substance, and style of the evangelistic preaching of Jesus. Twenty percent of the New Testament is composed of the actual words of Christ. According to Ralph and Greg Lewis, the total recorded words of Jesus "would equal approximately ten thirty-minute sermons" (Lewis, 13).

Preach a Communicated Gospel

The first corollary is the minister must preach in order to communicate the gospel. Teaching is not simply talking. Learning is not simply listening. What does it mean to communicate? The term *communication* comes from the Latin word *communis,* meaning "common." Commonness or commonality must first be established before effective communication can take place between people (Hendricks, 98). The more the messenger builds a commonality between the message and the listeners, the higher the level of communication between himself or herself and the audience. It is the responsibility of the evangelist and pastor to make sure the audience understands and applies the message to their lives. "True biblical teaching doesn't take place unless the students have learned" (Wilkinson, 26). But what does it mean to teach and learn? Are these concepts related?

When Moses spoke to his people in Deuteronomy, he used "teach" (4:1) and "learn" (5:1) in his message. Yet, in the Hebrew language, the same term for "learn" is used in an intensive form for "teach." He did not separate teaching and learning. How can evangelists know if they are effectively communicating the gospel? They can know by what the audience learns and applies to their lives (Wilkinson, 26–27).

There must be a balance between beginning with the needs of the people and the precepts of Scripture. On the one hand, people determine the starting point of the sermon. On the other hand, the Scripture determines the subject and substance of the sermon. This is not abdicating the supremacy of Scripture or the biblical basis for the sermon. This simply underscores the simple truth that ministers must begin where people are and not expect people to first come up to their level.

> **Commonality must be in place before effective communication can occur.**

In John 4, Jesus went to Samaria to preach the gospel. The conversation of Jesus with the woman at the well is an excellent model for preachers who wish to communicate the gospel effectively. Even though Evangelist Ron Hutchcraft has established this model for ministers, I would like to build upon it. Jesus had come into this world "to seek and save that which was lost" (Luke 19:10). Just as Jesus could not reach the Samaritans by preaching the gospel in Jerusalem, evangelists and pastors cannot preach evangelistically unless they are committed to "communicating" the gospel. According to Ron Hutchcraft, sermonizers must be willing to communicate the gospel to a given audience "on their turf . . . in their people group . . . in their language" (Hutchcraft, 58–59). Evangelistic preaching requires the minister to speak in a language that can be understood. Evangelists and pastors "have to translate the Gospel, not just transmit it" (Hutchcraft, 59). "Christianese" is a foreign language in post-Christian America, and translation is difficult in a constantly changing culture.

Preach a Connected Gospel

The second corollary is the minister must preach in order to connect the gospel. The preacher must have a point of contact with the audience. If there is no contact during the sermon, there most likely will be no response to the invitation. The point of contact for Jesus with the woman at the well in Samaria was "Give me a drink" (John 4:7). He began with His physical thirst before moving to her spiritual thirst (Hutchcraft, 60). What are the points of contact for evangelists and pastors today? What is the bridge between moral absolutes and the "doctrine of tolerance" in America? Ron Hutchcraft has profoundly observed:

> While most lost people do not care much about sin, they care very much about the results of sin. They have seen and experi-

enced the damage of sin without knowing it is sin that caused it. If we start with life issues they care about and a sin-symptom they struggle with, we can lead them to the cross (Hutchcraft, 60).

Preaching evangelistically like Jesus means beginning the sermon with the life issues of the audience. Evangelists and pastors are responsible for bringing the physical and spiritual needs of the congregation together. They must cause people to learn.

Jesus engaged His listeners. He used stories, dialogue, questions, comparisons and contrasts, common experiences, creativity, metaphors, and imagination to connect the gospel to His generation. Jesus went "from the concrete to the abstract, from the facts to the principles, from the data to the dictum" (Lewis, 27).

The evangelistic preaching of Jesus scratched where people itched in everyday life. Ralph and Greg Lewis have provided a list of Jesus' preaching topics. Jesus spoke on

adultery, anger, anxiety, avarice, death, debts, doubts, eternity, faith, fasting, fault-finding, giving, greed, honesty, hypocrisy, joy, kindness, knowledge, law, legalism, life, lust, marriage, money, oaths, parenthood, prayer, pretense, respect, responsibility, reward, rulers, sex, slander, speech, stewardship, taxes, trust, unkindness, virtue, wisdom, and zeal (Lewis, 29).

Furthermore, Jesus connected with His hearers by the stories, or parables (illustrations), He told them. According to Mark 4:34, "He did not speak to them without a parable." A descriptive story turns ears into eyes so people can see the truth in everyday life. Thirty-three percent of all the recorded teachings of Christ were parables, or stories (Lewis, 86). However, ministers must be cautioned not to make the basis of their sermons contemporary stories. Stories move people, but the Word of God changes people. Again, there must be a biblical balance between the open-ended inductive approach and the deductive approach for the development of evangelistic sermons.

Moreover, for culturally-relevant evangelists and pastors to persuade their listeners to believe the gospel, they must build a bridge between not only the spiritual and the physical but also the spiritual and mental. Learning involves the brain, which has a dual nature: "The left side deals more with facts, the right side more with feelings. The left with the rational, the right with the relational" (Lewis, 38). The left side thinks in principles while the right side thinks in pictures.

Jesus used memory, imagination, nature, and experience to paint word pictures on the canvas of the minds of His audience. How do the majority of people learn? They learn by perceiving (on the right half of the brain) and processing information (on the left half of the brain). Word pictures connect both halves of the brain (Lewis, 48–50). W. Macneile Dixon was astute in his conclusion: "The human mind is not, as philosophers would have you think, a debating hall, but a picture gallery" (Wiersbe, 24).

Jesus is the main issue in the evangelistic sermon.

The evangelistic preaching ministry of Jesus involved

both the left and right brain of His listeners. While most of our evangelistic preaching uses the left side of the mind, Jesus used mostly the right side of the mind. In essence, persuasive evangelistic preaching causes the right and left halves of the brain to focus simultaneously on the gospel. Left-brain evangelistic preaching answers the question, "What is the point?" Right-brain evangelistic preaching answers the question, "What is the picture?" "Whole brain" evangelistic preaching answers the question, "What is the package for the people?" When the "package" (vocabulary, style, dialogue, stories, comparisons and contrasts, imagination, life experiences, metaphors, technology, etc.) and the "product" (the gospel) are correctly synthesized, there is a connection made between the evangelist and his hearers.

Preach a Christ-Centered Gospel

The third corollary is the minister must preach a Christ-centered gospel. The apostle Paul declared to the Corinthians, "I determined to know nothing among you except Jesus Christ, and Him crucified" (1 Cor. 2:2). Philip preached Jesus Christ to the Samaritans (Acts 8:5,12) and to the Ethiopian eunuch (Acts 8:35). The Seventy preached the kingdom of God in the name of Jesus (Luke 10:9,11,17). Peter proclaimed "peace through Jesus Christ" to Cornelius and his household (Acts 10:36). The central thrust of the fivefold ministries of Ephesians 4:11–16 is the maturing of the body of Jesus Christ. Jesus is not simply another issue in the evangelistic sermon; He is the main issue in the evangelistic sermon.

When the woman at the well wanted to talk about religious matters relating to the worship of God, Jesus directed her thoughts back to himself, the Messiah (John 4:24–26). She came face to face with the realization that Jesus was the Son of God. He is the Christ (John 4:29). Evangelistic preaching crystallizes Jesus in the minds of people. "Christ should not be clouded by Christianity" (Hutchcraft, 62).

Preach a Confirmed Gospel

The fourth corollary is the evangelist must preach to confirm the gospel. Evangelistic preaching involves the anointing of the Holy Spirit upon the preacher. In Jesus' first sermon, He said:

> The Spirit of the Lord is upon Me, because He anointed Me to preach the gospel to the poor, He has sent Me to proclaim release to the captives, and recovery of sight to the blind, to set free those who are downtrodden, to proclaim the favorable year of the Lord (Luke 4:18–19).

Jesus announced to the congregation that He was called to preach the gospel. "The Holy Spirit is the calling agent of the church. He alone has the prerogative of appointing men to preach the glorious gospel of Christ" (Perry, 18). The goal of Jesus was simple: to preach the gospel effectively through the power of the Holy Spirit for the salvation of the lost.

According to Perry and Strubhar, there is a threefold strategic role of the Holy Spirit in the sermon preparation of the evangelist. First, the Holy Spirit is the "producer" (inspiration) of the Word of God (2 Tim. 3:16–17; 2 Pet. 1:20–21). Second, the Holy Spirit is the "penetrator" of the minister of God. The Holy Spirit opens the mind (illumination) of the preacher so proper interpretation and application can be made to the people. Third, the Holy Spirit is the "provider" of the minister's authority during the actual preaching of the gospel (Perry, 21–23). There can be no doubt that the Holy Spirit confirmed the message and ministry of Jesus Christ. The gospels are filled with miracles and transformed lives. Without the conscious anointing of the Holy Spirit upon the life and ministry of the preacher, there will be no long-lasting fruit in the local church.

Preach a Continued Gospel

The fifth corollary is the minister should preach to continue the gospel. The end result of a salvation sermon is not decisions for Christ but disciples for Christ (see chapter 8). Evangelists are often portrayed as loggers cutting down trees and pastors as craftsmen designing furniture out of the wood. Even though there is an element of truth in this unique evangelist-pastor relationship, the result of the soul-winning message is "changed lives."

Evangelistic preaching should ultimately produce evangelists who will carry the gospel to their respective people groups. This concept is often neglected in traditional homiletical textbooks. The task of the communicator "is not to impress people, but to impact them; not just to convince them, but to change them" (Hendricks, 77). In John 4:39, Jesus Christ knew "the most effective way to reach Samaritans was to have a Samaritan become an evangelist" (Hutchcraft, 62). New Testament evangelistic preaching does more than produce a "great moment of evangelism," it fosters a "great movement of evangelism" (Hutchcraft, 62).

Is our evangelistic preaching ministry leaving behind an army of evangelizers in the local church and community? Are we focusing on what we produce or what we reproduce? Success requires a successor. Is it not time for the evangelist to preach for results like that of Jesus?

INVITATION

The final step upward to the pulpit of proclamation is the *invitation*. The invitation phase is listed last because it is viewed as taking place at the end of the sermon. However, effective preachers begin their invitations in the interpretation phase, looking for bridges of persuasion. The end is viewed from the beginning.

What is an invitation? Street defines it as follows:

> The invitation is that act by which the preacher of the gospel exhorts his hearers and instructs them how to appropriate the content of the *kerygma* in their individual lives. Any sermon that does not include an invitation as well as a proclamation is not New Testament-style preaching. Every sermon should aim to stir the human will. Truth is something that must be obeyed. It is the gospel invitation that presses home the claims of Christ and calls for an immediate response (Street, 37).

Just as the first-century minister concluded the message with an invitation for people to repent of sin and place their faith in the Lord Jesus Christ for salvation, the twenty-first-century minister should strive to invite people at the close of the sermon to come to Christ for eternal life.

Why should a preacher give a public invitation? There are at least six reasons. First, the invitation is biblical. The Old and New Testaments are filled with invitations from God, Christ, the prophets, apostles, and evangelists. Second, invitations are psychological. Whitsell explains:

> Emotions aroused and desires stirred will soon pass away unless acted upon at once. Good impulses are harder to generate the second time than they were the first time if the first impulse did not result in action (Whitsell, 17).

Third, the invitation is historical. Church history is filled with examples of the effectiveness of the public invitation. Famous evangelists in the annals of church history were masters at giving persuasive, public invitations. Fourth, invitations are salvational. They aid in bringing people to Jesus Christ. Fifth, invitations are logical. If evangelists and pastors are willing to instruct people regarding the salvation of their soul, then they should logically extend an invitation to experience forgiveness of sin immediately. Sixth, invitations are spiritual. They are spiritual both for the preacher and the audience. The preacher must depend upon the convicting presence of the Holy Spirit, and the lost must express their spiritual need of Christ.

How does a preacher prepare and give an effective public invitation? For an invitation to be persuasive, it must "be tied in closely with the major thrust of the sermon. . . . In other words, it should grow out of the main theme of the message so that the people will not be surprised when it is given" (Perry, 113). It should also be implicit throughout the sermon to prepare people for their response. The effective minister looks for ways to imply the invitation throughout the entire development of the evangelistic message. Much practice comes before the presentation of powerful invitations.

What characterizes an effective invitation? Evangelists

are to present invitations clearly, confidently, compassionately, courageously, courteously, earnestly, positively, honestly, prayerfully, dependently on the Holy Spirit, passionately, scripturally, faithfully, expectantly, friendly, repeatedly, and resourcefully.

To prepare and deliver an effective invitation, the evangelist and pastor must pray, use appropriate transitions leading into the invitation and away from the main body of the sermon, persuade ethically, extend a public call, and be led by the Holy Spirit.

When should a minister issue an invitation? The natural response is, At the end of the message. However, the "supernatural" response is, When the Holy Spirit wants the evangelist to begin and conclude the invitation. Timing is crucial to presenting an effective, life-changing invitation to people.

The Phases of 21st-Century

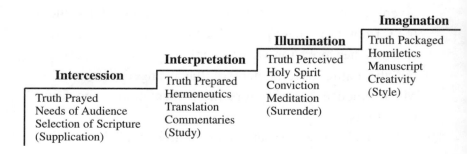

Imagination

Truth Packaged
Homiletics
Manuscript
Creativity
(Style)

Illumination

Truth Perceived
Holy Spirit
Conviction
Meditation
(Surrender)

Interpretation

Truth Prepared
Hermeneutics
Translation
Commentaries
(Study)

Intercession

Truth Prayed
Needs of Audience
Selection of Scripture
(Supplication)

However, the evangelist and pastor must not forget to allow enough time for the invitation to be issued and for the Holy Spirit to work in the hearts of the lost. Why take the time to proceed through the phases of intercession, interpretation, illumination, imagination, illustration, introduction, impartation, and invitation and not allow enough time for people to repent of their sins and believe in Jesus Christ? The diagram below crystallizes the eight steps to effective evangelistic preaching for the twenty-first-century evangelist.

The Presentation of Evangelistic Preaching

The pulpit is no greater than the minister who fills it. If the evangelist or pastor is boring to the congregation, then the people will think God is boring. Some preachers have style without substance while others have substance without

Evangelistic Preaching

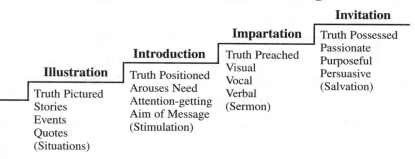

Illustration

Truth Pictured
Stories
Events
Quotes
(Situations)

Introduction

Truth Positioned
Arouses Need
Attention-getting
Aim of Message
(Stimulation)

Impartation

Truth Preached
Visual
Vocal
Verbal
(Sermon)

Invitation

Truth Possessed
Passionate
Purposeful
Persuasive
(Salvation)

style. Preachers need to be able to combine substance with style in their preaching today. The Christian and non-Christian alike are searching for truth in a generation preoccupied with self, acquisition, and gratification.

Substance is what is said and style is how it is said. There is a certain amount of style in the packaging of a sermon. In John 12:49 Jesus said, "I did not speak on My own initiative, but the Father Himself who sent Me has given Me commandment, what to say, and what to speak." In other words, Jesus was led by the Father in all aspects of His speaking engagements.

In this section the focus is on the actual delivery of the evangelistic sermon. What do we mean by the delivery of a sermon? It simply means to deliver "into the possession of the person for whom it was intended" (Brown, 155). "Delivery refers to the methods by which you communicate 'what' you have to say to the 'who'" (Arredondo, 65). Many souls are not saved because the sermon was never delivered to the lost. It is possible for the evangelist to speak the message, use up a portion of time, give an altar call, and still not accomplish the intended purpose of the evangelistic sermon.

The evangelistic message is delivered through the means of the "verbal," "vocal," and "visual" (Arredondo, 65). Many ministers spend most of their time thinking about what they are going to say to the nightly audience. Yet, studies have concluded that the decision-making process of people is determined first by visual cues (55 percent), second by vocal cues (sounds and tones account for 38 percent), and third by verbal cues (actual words of the presentation account for only 7 percent). This data proves that the average person is persuaded more by feelings than by facts.

The visual cues a preacher gives to the audience are positively or negatively persuasive. Mannerisms, gestures, head movements, facial expressions, platform movement, eye contact, and clothing project the overall presence of the evangelist.

The vocal effectiveness of the preacher is determined by quality, intonation, pauses, and fillers (Arredondo, 77–79). The voice should project the different "landscapes" of the sermon. There should be changes in volume, speed, and tone according to the content of the message. Pauses help the minister and the audience catch up with the message. Fillers should be avoided at all cost.

The verbal persuasion of the evangelist and pastor will be greatly determined by the choice of words and phrases. Emotive words drive home the theme of the message. Since only 7 percent of the impact in the decision-making process of people is made of the actual words, every word and phrase of the itinerant should be chosen carefully for maximum impact. We must always remember we are not called merely to impress people but to influence their decision making for Christ. If a minister is saying one thing but the voice is saying another, confusion will result in the minds of the congregation.

Just like there are unique styles of clothing to cover our physical bodies, there are unique styles of communication to clothe our thoughts. Charles Brown has put it this way:

> You cannot send your ideas out naked—they will refuse to go if they have any shred of modesty about them, and people will refuse to welcome them into good society if they undertake to make their approach in such an unseemly way (Brown, 177).

One of the best ways to develop a dynamic preaching style is by writing out the sermon. When doing so, write it for the ear and not the eye. Ask yourself, "Does this sermon sound right?" While thinking about the message will make the evangelist creative, writing out the sermon will make the evangelist exact.

Know your audience at all times during the preaching of the sermon. This is crucial to effectiveness. A sermon is not too long because the clock says so. It is too long if the audience says so. If you are wondering if the congregation is following you, walk to the outskirts of the platform and watch the heads of the people. If their heads turn as you walk, they are with you. However, if the people refuse to follow you, you need to conclude the sermon as quickly as possible.

Here are some additional suggestions regarding style: (1) never read from or memorize a manuscript, (2) never speak in an angry tone, (3) never point at people, (4) never embarrass people, (5) respect people and their time, (6) view yourself as a role model, (7) say thank you for having the opportunity to speak to them, and (8) start and finish on time.

Evangelism Exercises

1. What is the best picture of evangelistic preaching? Describe it.
2. What is the ultimate purpose of a sermon?
3. What are the six precepts of evangelistic preaching? How do each of these precepts apply to your ministry?
4. What are the seven steps to developing effective evangelistic messages? Which step is the most difficult one for you? Spend the next thirty days improving this step in your sermon preparation.
5. What are the five corollaries of communicating the gospel? Describe each one and apply it to your preaching.
6. What are the differences between style and substance? On which one do you focus the most? How can you accomplish both in your presentation of the gospel?
7. How can you apply the findings about visual, vocal, and verbal cues to your present ministry? Play a video recording of you preaching a sermon. For the next three months, strengthen each of these elements by focusing on one of them per month.

Conclusion

We live in a reachable world. If this is true, why has the Church failed to evangelize the world after two thousand years? The lack of world evangelization is not due to the size of the world, a growing population, false religions, political systems, or cultural barriers. When the Lord Jesus Christ was on earth, He did not plan for himself to reach the world with the gospel. The Master's plan (see Robert Coleman) was to equip His disciples for world evangelization. The Church has not accomplished the Great Commission because we have failed to equip both the minister and parishioner for evangelism and discipleship. Equipping is the answer.

For too long, the Church has endeavored to reach the world through addition and division instead of by multiplication. For example, if an evangelist had the physical stamina to preach every night to a crowd of fifty thousand people and witnessed at least one thousand conversions in each service for thirty-four years, he would win more than one million people to Christ. He would have conducted the greatest revival in church history.

However, if that same evangelist discipled just one person for evangelism in one year, and that person and the evangelist each discipled one more person each for evangelism during the next year, there would be four people equipped as evangelists or lay evangelists after two years. If each of these four discipled one new person, there would be eight evangelists or lay evangelists trained for evangelism at the end of three years. At first, this would seem to be a much slower process of world evangelization. However, after thirty-four years where each one discipled a new evangelist or lay evangelist each year, the total number of conversions would be more than sixteen billion! We live in a reachable world.

Open-air and citywide crusades are effective tools for winning the lost. Local church campaigns are still vital in the overall life of the church. Biblical revivals turn saints into soul-winners. Spiritual awakenings cause cities and sometimes entire nations to turn to God. In each of these events, evangelists have led the way in cutting-edge evangelism. New Testament evangelists know how to surf the spiritual waves of revival for the purpose of evangelism and discipleship. Will the rest of the world be told the gospel? If not now, then when? If the evan-

Will the world be told the gospel? If the evangelist will not lead the way, then who will?

gelists will not lead the way, then who will?

Evangelists have been called by Christ to equip the Church in evangelism. Just like the other ministry gifts, evangelists are to multiply themselves in the Church for the purpose of world evangelization. Evangelists and evangelism go hand in hand.

Since this is part of Christ's plan for world evangelization, how can evangelists and pastors grow effective evangelistic ministries in a rapidly changing world? This is not an easy task either for the beginner or the more advanced evangelist. Rick Warren writes about growing a church by comparing it to a Chinese bamboo tree.

> Of all the growth patterns I've observed as a gardener, the growth of the Chinese bamboo tree is the most amazing to me. Plant a bamboo sprout in the ground, and for four or five years (sometimes much longer) nothing happens! You water and fertilize, water and fertilize, water and fertilize—but you see no visible evidence that anything is happening. Nothing! But about the fifth year things change rather dramatically. In a six-week period the Chinese bamboo tree grows to be a staggering ninety feet tall! *World Book Encyclopedia* records that one bamboo plant can grow three feet in a single twenty-four hour period (Warren, 391–92).

Developing a full-time, evangelistic preaching ministry is a lot like growing bamboo trees. For the first five years, there will usually not be much visible evidence of long-term effectiveness in the church and world. Both parishioners and ministers alike may not recognize young, gifted leadership for evangelism. However, if these evangelists and pastors will keep watering and fertilizing their ministry, the day will come when their ministries will burst forth with new opportunities for evangelistic leadership in the church at large.

I have endeavored to prescribe the biblical, spiritual, and practical fertilizers necessary to grow an effective evangelistic preaching ministry. You will have to take the initiative to add the water of prayer, patience, and pruning on a daily basis. This book has logically outlined the pattern for birthing, building, and broadening a full-time evangelistic preaching ministries. We now end where we began.

Have your evangelism efforts become root-bound like redwood trees stuffed into flowerpots? Do you have a root-bound ministry? If so, then replanting is necessary for world evangelization. Is your ministry growing on an annual basis? Are you fulfilling God's purpose for your life in this generation? In the twenty-first century, will evangelists lead the church in evangelism, or will they be led by others? My sincere purpose in writing this book is to equip evangelists for evangelism and pastors to "do the work of the evangelist" so they can in turn equip others for evangelism. If this will be the result in their evangelism efforts, then my God-given goal has been actualized for the cause of Christ.

Reference List

Achtemeir, Elizabeth. 1980. *Creative Preaching.* Nashville: Abingdon.

Aldrich, Joseph C. 1981. *Lifestyle Evangelism.* Portland, Oregon: Multnomah Press.

Archibald, Arthur C. 1946. *New Testament Evangelism.* Philadelphia: Judson Press.

Armerding, Hudson T. 1978. *Leadership.* Wheaton, Illinois: Tyndale.

Armstrong, Richard Stoll. 1984. *The Pastor As Evangelist.* Philadelphia: Westminster Press.

Arredondo, Lani. 1991. *How To Present Like a Pro: Getting People to See Things Your Way.* New York: Mcgraw-Hill.

Autrey, C. E. 1954. *The Theology of Evangelism.* Grand Rapids, Michigan: Zondervan.

Avens, Robert. 1980. *Imagination Is Reality.* Dallas: Spring Publications.

Barker, Joel. 1992. *Future Edge.* New York: Morrow.

Barna, George. 1993. A Survey of the Training Needs and Interests of Itinerant Evangelists in North America. Tms [photocopy]. n.p.

Baumann, J. Daniel. 1972. *An Introduction to Contemporary Preaching.* Grand Rapids, Michigan: Baker.

Beecher, Henry Ward. 1872. *Yale's Lectures on Preaching.* New York: J. B. Ford and Company.

Bennis, Warren. 1994. *On Becoming a Leader.* New York: Addison-Wesley.

Bennis, Warren, and Robert Townsend. 1995. *Reinventing Leadership.* New York: Morrow.

Beougher, Timothy, and Alvin Ried, ed. 1995. *Evangelism for a Changing World.* Wheaton, Illinois: Harold Shaw Publishers.

Biederwolf, William E. 1921. *Evangelism: Its Justification, Its Operation, and Its Value.* New York: Revell.

Blanchard, Ken and Sheldon Bowles. 1993. *Raving Fans.* New York: Morrow.

Blanchard, Ken and Terry Waghorn. 1996. *Mission Possible: Becoming a World-Class Organization While There's Still Time.* New York: McGraw-Hill.

Bounds, E. M. 1993. *Powerful and Prayerful Pulpit.* Grand Rapids, Michigan: Baker.

Bright, Bill. 1995. *The Coming Revival: America's Call to Fast, and Pray, and Seek God's Face.* Orlando, Florida: New Life.

Broadus, John A. 1979. *On the Preparation and the Delivery of Sermons.* 4th ed. San Francisco: Harper and Row.

Brooks, Peter. 1983. *Communicating Conviction.* London: Epworth Press.

Brown, Charles Reynolds. 1922. *The Art of Preaching.* New York: Macmillan.

Brown, Stanley C. 1963. *Evangelism in the Early Church.* Grand Rapids, Michigan: Eerdmans.

Bruce, F. F. 1980. *Commentary on the Book of Acts.* Grand Rapids, Michigan: Eerdmans.

_____. 1984. *The Epistles to the Colossians, to Philemon, and to the Ephesians.* Grand Rapids, Michigan: Eerdmans.

Brumback, Carl. 1961. *Suddenly . . . From Heaven.* Springfield, Missouri: Gospel Publishing House.

Buford, Bob. 1994. *Half Time: Changing Your Game Plan From Success to Significance.* Grand Rapids, Michigan: Zondervan.

Bugg, Charles B. 1992. *Preaching from the Inside Out.* Nashville: Broadman.

Buttrick, David. 1994. *A Captive Voice.* Louisville, Kentucky: Westminster/John Knox Press.

Buttrick, George A. 1970. *Jesus Came Preaching.* 2d ed. Grand Rapids, Michigan: Baker.

Burns, James. 1960. *Revivals: Their Laws and Leaders.* Grand Rapids, Michigan: Baker.

Byham, William C., and Jeff Cox. 1988. *Zapp!: The Lightning of Empowerment.* New York: Fawcett Columbine.

Chaney, Charles L., and Granville Watson. 1993. *Evangelism: Today and Tomorrow.* Nashville: Broadman.

Coleman, Robert. 1981. *The Master Plan of Evangelism.* 30th anniversary ed. Old Tappan, New Jersey: Revell.

_____. 1986. *Evangelism on the Cutting Edge.* Old Tappan, New Jersey: Revell.

Coulson, John. 1981. *Religion and Imagination.* Oxford: The Clarendon.

Covey, Stephen R. 1989. *The Seven Habits of Highly Effective People.* New York: Simon and Schuster.

_____. 1990. *Principle-Centered Leadership.* New York: Simon and Schuster.

_____. 1994. *First Things First.* New York: Simon and Schuster.

Craddock, Fred B. 1985. *Preaching.* Nashville: Abingdon.

_____. 1990. *Luke.* Louisville, Kentucky: John Knox Press.

Dale, R. W. 1986. *Nine Lectures on Preaching.* London: Hodder and Stoughton.

Dixon, John W., Jr. 1978. *Art and the Theological Imagination.* New York: Seabury.

Dorries, David W. 1992. "The Making of Smith Wigglesworth—Part 1: The Making of the Man." *Assemblies of God Heritage,* 12 (Fall): 4–8, 32.

_____. 1992. "The Making of Smith Wigglesworth—Part 2: The Making of His Message." *Assemblies of God Heritage,* 12 (Winter): 22, 29.

Douglas, J. D. 1984. *The Work of the Evangelist.* Minneapolis: World Wide Publications.

Drummond, Lewis. 1975. *Leading Your Church into Evangelism.* Nashville: Broadman.

_____. 1987. *The Calling of the Evangelist.* Minneapolis: World Wide Publications.

_____. 1996. *Biblical Affirmations for Evangelism.* Minneapolis: World Wide Publications.

_____. 1996. *Biblical Standards for Itinerant Evangelists.* Minneapolis: World Wide Publications.

Duewel, Wesley L. 1995. *Revival Fire.* Grand Rapids, Michigan: Zondervan.

Egan, Kieran. 1992. *Imagination in Teaching and Learning.* Chicago: University of Chicago.

Elwell, Walter A., ed. 1984. *Evangelical Dictionary of Theology.* Grand Rapids, Michigan: Baker.

Ervin, Howard M. 1984. *Conversion-Initiation and the Baptism in the Holy Spirit.* Peabody, Massachusetts: Hendrickson Publishers.

Evans, Craig A. 1990. *Luke.* Peabody, Massachusetts: Hendrickson Publishers.

Finney, Charles G. 1988. *Lectures on Revival and Religion.* New York: Revell.

Finzel, Hans. 1994. *The Top Ten Mistakes Leaders Make.* Wheaton, Illinois: Victor.

Fish, Roy J. 1974. *Giving an Effective Invitation.* Nashville: Broadman.

Fletcher, Lionel B. 1923. *The Effective Evangelist.* London: Hodder and Stoughton.

Flynn, Leslie B. 1987. *Come Alive with Illustrations.* Grand Rapids, Michigan: Baker.

Foulkes, Francis. 1989. *Ephesians.* 2d ed. Leicester, England: Inter-Varsity.

Freeman, Harold. 1987. *Variety in Biblical Preaching.* Waco, Texas: Word Books.

Friedrich, Erlangen Hauck. 1964. *Evaggelistes.* In *Theological Dictionary of the New Testament,* ed. Kittel, Gerhard, 2:737. Grand Rapids, Michigan: Eerdmans.

Frye, Northrop. 1964. *The Educated Imagination.* Bloomington: Indiana University Press.

Frye, Northrop. 1990. *Words with Power.* New York: Harcourt Brace Jovanovich.

Geldenhuys, Norval. 1983. *Commentary on the Gospel of Luke.* Grand Rapids, Michigan: Eerdmans.

Ghiselin, Brewster, ed. 1985. *The Creative Process.* Berkeley: University of California.

Gohr, Glenn. 1991. "Bert Webb: A Man Used by God." *Assemblies of God Heritage,* 11 (Fall):16–18.

_____. 1991. "Bert Webb: A Man Used by God." *Assemblies of God Heritage,* 11 (Winter): 19–20.

_____. 1996. "Carl W. Barnes: Evangelist, Song Leader, Church Builder." *Assemblies of God Heritage* 16 (Spring): 6–10, 29–30.

_____. 1996. "J. Robert Ashcroft: A Man of Prayer and Faith." *Assemblies of God Heritage,* 16 (Summer): 21–22, 50.

Graham, Billy. 1984. *A Biblical Standard for Evangelists.* Minneapolis: World Wide Publications.

Grant, Steve. 1996. "C. M. Ward: Voice of the Assemblies of God for 25 Years." *Assemblies of God Heritage* (Summer): 16.

Green, Michael. 1970. *Evangelism in the Early Church.* London: Hodden & Stoughton.

Greenleaf, Robert K. 1996. *On Becoming A Servant Leader.* San Francisco: Jossey-Bass Publishers.

Greidanus, Sidney. 1988. *The Modern Preacher and the Ancient Text.* Grand Rapids, Michigan: Eerdmans.

Gruden, Robert. 1990. *The Grace of Great Things: Creativity and Innovation.* New York: Ticknor and Fields.

Guthrie, Donald. 1981. *New Testament Theology.* Downers Grove, Illinois: Inter-Varsity Press.

Haenchen, Ernst. 1971. *The Acts of the Apostles.* Translated by R. McL. Wilson. Philadelphia: Westminster Press.

Harrell, Jr., David Edwin. 1975. *All Things Are Possible: The Healing and Charismatic Revivals in Modern America.* Bloomington: Indiana University Press.

Hawkes, Terence. 1972. *Metaphor.* London: Methuen.

Hendricks, Howard G. 1987. *Teaching to Change Lives.* Portland, Oregon: Multnomah Press.

Hendricks, Howard and William Hendricks. 1994. *As Iron Sharpens Iron.* Chicago: Moody.

Hendricksen, William. 1967. *New Testament Commentary: Exposition of Ephesians.* Grand Rapids, Michigan: Baker.

_____. 1980. *Commentary on 1 and 2 Timothy.* Grand Rapids, Michigan: Baker.

Hesselbein, Frances, and Marshall Goldsmith, and Richard Beckhard, eds. 1996. *The Leader of the Future.* San Francisco: Jossey-Bass.

Hoff, Ron. 1992. *I Can See You Naked.* Kansas City, Missouri: Andrews and McMeel.

Holmes, Urban T., III. 1976. *Ministry and Imagination.* New York: Seabury.

Hull, William E. 1992. "The Contemporary World and the Preaching Task." In *Handbook of Contemporary Preaching,* ed. Michael Duduit, 571–83. Nashville: Broadman.

Hunter, George G. 1992. *How to Reach Secular People.* Nashville: Abingdon Press.

Hutchcraft, Ronald. 1996. "Relating the Gospel to a Secular Society." In *Equipping for Evangelism,* ed. Lewis A. Drummond, 131–47. Minneapolis: World Wide Publications.

Huttar, Charles, ed. 1971. *Imagination and the Spirit.* Grand Rapids, Michigan: Baker.

Johnson, Bernhard. 1995. "Standing Strong in the Battle." *Pentecostal Evangel,* no. 4226, May 1995, 62.

Jones, Laurie Beth. 1995. *Jesus CEO.* New York: Hyperion.

_____. 1996. *The Path.* New York: Hyperion.

Kendall, R. T. 1985. *Stand Up and Be Counted: Calling for a Public Confession of Faith.* Grand Rapids, Michigan: Zondervan.

Kennedy, D. James. 1996. 4th ed. *Evangelism Explosion.* Wheaton, Illinois: Tyndale.

Kirkpatrick, Robert White. 1944. *The Creative Delivery of Sermons.* New York: Macmillan.

Kriegel, Robert and David Brandt. 1996. *Sacred Cows Make the Best Hamburgers.* New York: Warner Books.

Kuhlman, Edward. 1987. *The Master Teacher.* Old Tappan, New Jersey: Revell.

Larsen, David. 1989. *The Anatomy of Preaching.* Grand Rapids, Michigan: Baker.

_____. 1992. *The Evangelism Mandate—Recovering the Centrality of Gospel Preaching.* Wheaton, Illinois: Crossway Books.

Larson, Brian, and Mark Galli. 1994. *Preaching That Connects.* Grand Rapids, Michigan: Zondervan.

Leckey, Andrew. 1997. *The Morning Star Approach to Investing: Wiring into the Mutual Fund Revolution.* New York: Warner Books.

Lenski, R. C. H. 1961. *The Interpretation of St. Paul's Epistles to the Galatians, to the Ephesians, and to the Philippians.* Vol 8. Minneapolis: Augsburg Publishing.

Lewis, David. 1996. *How to Get Your Message Across.* London: Souvenir Press.

Lewis, Ralph L., and Gregg Lewis. 1989. *Learning to Preach Like Jesus.* Wheaton, Illinois: Crossway Books.

Liefeld, Walter L. 1981. *Luke.* Vol. 8, *Expositor's Bible Commentary.* Grand Rapids, Michigan: Zondervan.

Lincoln, Andrew T. 1990. *Word Biblical Commentary: Ephesians.* Vol. 42. Dallas: Word.

Longenecker, Richard N. 1981. *Acts.* Vol. 9, *Expositor's Bible Commentary.* Grand Rapids, Michigan: Zondervan.

Loscalzo, Craig A. 1995. *Evangelistic Preaching That Connects.* Downers Grove, Illinois: Inter-Varsity Press.

MacArthur, John. 1986. *The MacArthur New Testament Commentary: Ephesians.* Chicago: Moody.

_____. 1992. *Rediscovering Expository Preaching.* Waco, Texas: Word Books.

McClellan, Jimmy. 1996. "A Church Is Born in Goose Creek, Texas." *Assemblies of God Heritage,* 16 (Summer): 16.

McKenna, David L. 1990. *The Coming Great Awakening.* Downers Grove, Illinois: InterVarsity.

McLaughlin, Raymond W. 1979. *The Ethics of Persuasive Preaching.* Grand Rapids, Michigan: Baker.

Marshall, Howard I. 1983. *The Acts of the Apostles.* Grand Rapids, Michigan: Eerdmans.

Maxwell, John C. 1993. *The Winning Attitude.* Nashville: Nelson Publishers.

_____. 1994. *Developing the Leader Within You.* Nashville: Nelson Publishers.

_____. 1995. *Developing Leaders Around You.* Nashville: Nelson Publishers.

_____. 1997. *The Success Journey.* Nashville: Nelson Publishers.

Menzies, Robert P. 1991. *The Development of Early Christian Pneumatology.* Sheffield, England: Sheffield Academic Press.

Menzies, William W. 1971. *Anointed to Serve.* Springfield, Missouri: Gospel Publishing House.

Michel, Tubingen Otto. 1967. *Oikos.* In *Theological Dictionary of the New Testament,* ed. Kittel Gerhard, 5: 119–59. Grand Rapids, Michigan: Eerdmans.

Morris, Canon Leon. 1983. *The Gospel According to Luke.* Grand Rapids, Michigan: Eerdmans.

Murray, Iain H. 1994. *Revival & Revivalism: The Making and Marring of American Evangelicalism.* Edinburg, England: The Banner of Truth Trust.

Novak, Michael. 1996. *Business as a Calling: Work and the Examined Life.* New York: Free Press.

Osborne, Grant R. 1991. *The Hermeneutical Spiral.* Downers Grove, Illinois: InterVarsity Press.

Palmer, Richard E. 1969. *Hermeneutics.* Evanston, Illinois: Northwestern University.

Patterson, Ben. 1996. "Preaching and Prayer." In *Communicate With Power,* ed. Michael Duduit, 150–55. Grand Rapids, Michigan: Baker.

Pattison, T. Harwood. 1898. *The Making of the Sermon.* Philadelphia: The American Baptist Publications Society.

Patzia, Arthur G. 1990. *Ephesians, Colossians, Philemon.* Peabody, Massachusetts: Hendrickson Publishers.

Paul, John. 1995. "Essentials of an Evangelist." Dmin. diss., Trinity Evangelical Divinity School.

Perry, Lloyd M. 1973. *Biblical Preaching for Today's World.* Chicago: Moody.

Perry, Lloyd M., and John R. Strubhar. 1979. *Evangelistic Preaching.* Chicago: Moody.

Phillips, Donald. 1992. *Lincoln on Leadership.* New York: Warner Books.

Phillips, John. 1986. *Exploring Acts.* Vol 1. Chicago: Moody.

Phillips, Tom. 1995. *Revival Signs: Join the Spiritual Awakening.* Gresham, Oregon: Vision House.

Powell, Ivor. 1965. *Luke's Thrilling Gospel.* Grand Rapids, Michigan: Kregel.

_____. 1987. *The Amazing Acts.* Grand Rapids, Michigan: Kregel.

_____. 1989. *The Exciting Epistle to the Ephesians.* Grand Rapids, Michigan: Kregel.

Quayle, William A. 1910. *The Pastor-Preacher.* New York: Eaton and Mains.

Qubein, Nido R. 1997. *How to Be a Great Communicator.* New York: John Wiley and Sons.

_____. 1997. *Stairway to Success.* New York: John Wiley and Sons.

Rice, Charles L. 1970. *Interpretation and Imagination.* Philadelphia: Fortress.

Rice, John R. 1968. *The Evangelist and His Work.* Murfreesboro, Tennessee: Sword of the Lord Publishers.

Robinson, Haddon W. 1980. *Biblical Preaching.* Grand Rapids, Michigan: Baker.

Robinson, J. Armitage. 1979. *Commentary on Ephesians.* Grand Rapids, Michigan: Kregel.

Ryle, J. C. 1977. *Expository Thoughts on the Gospels.* Grand Rapids, Michigan: Baker.

Salter, Darius. 1996. *American Evangelism.* Grand Rapids, Michigan: Baker.

Schippers, Reinier. 1986. "Equipping." In *The New International Dictionary of New Testament Theology,* ed. Colon Brown, 3:349–51. Grand Rapids, Michigan: Eerdmans.

Sease, Douglas and John Prestbo. 1994. *Barrons: Guide to Making Investment Decisions.* Englewood Cliffs, New Jersey: Prentice Hall.

Simpson, Matthew. 1879. *Yale's Lectures on Preaching.* New York: Hunt and Eaton.

Smith, Hyrum W. 1994. *The Ten Natural Laws to Success and Life Management.* New York: Warner Books.

Spurgeon, Charles H. 1954. *Lectures to My Students.* Grand Rapids, Michigan: Zondervan.

Stinnett, Nick, ed. 1985. *Family Building: Six Qualities of a Strong Family.* Ventura, California: Regal.

Stott, John R. W. 1979. *God's New Society.* Downers Grove, Illinois: InterVarsity.

_____1961. *The Preacher's Portrait.* Grand Rapids, Michigan: Eerdmans.

_____1982. *Between Two Worlds.* Grand Rapids, Michigan: Eerdmans.

_____1990. *The Spirit, the Church, and the World.* Downers Grove, Illinois: Inter-Varsity.

Street, Alan R. 1984. *The Effective Invitation.* Old Tappan, New Jersey: Revell.

Stronstad, Roger. 1984. *The Charismatic Theology of Luke.* Peabody, Massachusetts: Hendrickson Publishers.

Sweazey, George E. 1953. *Effective Evangelism: The Greatest Work in the World.* New York: Harper and Brothers Publishers.

Sweeting, George. 1955. *The Evangelistic Camp.* Chicago: Moody.

Swenson, Richard A. 1992. *Margin: Restoring Emotional, Physical, Financial, and Time Reserves to Overloaded Lives.* Colorado Springs, Colorado: Navpress.

Tannehill, Robert C. 1990. *The Narrative Unity of Luke-Acts.* Vol. 2. Minneapolis: Fortress Press.

Taylor, Jack R. 1993. *The Word of God with Power.* Nashville: Broadman.

Tigue, Joseph and Joseph Lisanti. 1997. *The Dividend Rich Investor.* New York: McGraw Hill.

Torrey, R. A. 1901. *How to Promote and Conduct a Successful Revival.* New York: Revell.

Troeger, Thomas H. 1990. *Imagining a Sermon.* Nashville: Abingdon.

Vance, Mike and Diane Deacon. 1996. *Think Out of the Box.* Franklin Lakes, New Jersey: Career Press.

"Veteran religious broadcaster C. M. Ward dies at 87." *Pentecostal Evangel,* no. 4297, 15 September 1996, 23.

Vines, Jerry. 1985. *A Practical Guide to Sermon Preparation.* Chicago: Moody.

_____. 1986. *A Guide to Effective Sermon Delivery.* Chicago: Moody.

Waitley, Denis. 1985. *The Double Win.* Old Tappan, New Jersey: Revell.

_____. 1995. *Empires of the Mind.* New York: Morrow.

_____. 1996. *The New Dynamics of Goal Setting.* New York: Morrow.

Warner, Wayne. 1988. "Pioneering Churches in South Central Iowa." *Assemblies of God Heritage,* 8 (Spring): 8–10.

_____. 1988. "Hattie Hammond." In *Dictionary of Pentecostal and Charismatic Movements,* ed. Stanley M. Burgess and Gary B. McGee, 346. Grand Rapids, Michigan: Zondervan.

_____. 1996. "Determination in Yarbo, Alabama." *Assemblies of God Heritage,* 16 (Summer): 6–9.

_____. 1996. "A Legend Among Church Planters." *Assemblies of God Heritage,* 16 (Summer): 3–5.

Warren, Rick. 1995. *The Purpose-Driven Church: Growth Without Compromising Your Message and Mission.* Grand Rapids, Michigan: Zondervan.

Wiegold, Frederic C. 1997. *Lifetime Guide to Money.* New York: Dow Jones and Company.

White, Douglas M. 1984. *The Excellence of Exposition.* Neptune, New Jersey: Loizeaux Brothers.

Whitsell, F. D. 1984. *Sixty-Five Ways to Give an Evangelistic Invitation.* Grand Rapids, Michigan: Kregel.

Wiersbe, Warren W. 1994. *Preaching and Teaching with Imagination: The Quest for Biblical Preaching.* Wheaton, Illinois: Victor Books.

Wilkinson, Bruce H. 1992. *The Seven Laws of the Learner.* Sisters, Oregon: Multnomah Press.

Wilson, George, ed. 1969. *Evangelism Now.* Minneapolis: World Wide Publications.

Wilson, Paul Scott. 1988. *Imagination of the Heart—New Understanding in Preaching.* Nashville: Abingdon Press.

Wood, A. Skevington. 1981. *Ephesians.* Vol. 11, *Expositor's Bible Commentary.* Grand Rapids, Michigan: Zondervan.

Wright, Norman H. 1992. *Family Is Still a Great Idea.* Ann Arbor, Michigan: Vine Books.

Young, Robert D. 1979. *Religious Imagination: God's Gift to Prophets and Preachers.* Philadelphia: Westminster.

Scripture Index

New Testament

Subject Index

Samaritans receive, 156
Stephen filled with, 162
symbols of, 160–162
teaches meaning of Word,
181
See also Baptism in the
Spirit.
Homiletic, 172, 183–185, 197
Honorariums, 131

I ─────────────

Illumination, 180–181, 196
Illustration, 187, 194
Image, 137
Imagination, 176, 180–184,
187, 194
Incarnation, 170–171
Inductive study, 178–180,
190, 194
Inspiration, 170–171, 180,
196
Integrity of evangelists,
48, 56–57, 130
Intercession, 174
Interpretation, 175, 177–178,
181, 187, 197–198
Introduction, 188–189
Invitation, 152, 173, 192,
198–200
Itinerant, 175, 203

J ─────────────

James, 91
Jerusalem, 192
Jesus Christ
center of our preaching,
171–172

commission of Seventy, 53–
54, 56
example in prayer, 88
five corollaries in preaching, 190–197
ministry by faith, 142
promised Pentecost, 158
Spirit-filled Evangelist,
162, 189
taught disciples to pray, 174
trained others in
evangelism, 189
Joel, 158
John the Apostle, 60, 73
John the Baptist, 158, 189
Johnson, Bernhard, 30
Judgment, 172

K ─────────────

Kerygma, 37, 198

L ─────────────

Language, 192
Lausanne Covenant of
International Congress of
World Evangelism, 34
Laying on of hands, 60
Leader, 189
Leadership, 99–109, 210
Listener, 171, 176, 180, 182,
187, 190

M ─────────────

Manuscript, 204
Marketing, 135–137

DATE DUE / DATE DE RETOUR

CARR MᶜLEAN

38-297